Chen v. Miller

Case File
Trial Materials

CHEN V. MILLER

Case File
Trial Materials

Linda L. Lane
Professor of Practice
University of San Diego School of Law

NITA®
NATIONAL INSTITUTE FOR TRIAL ADVOCACY

Address inquiries to:
Reprint Permission
National Institute for Trial Advocacy
325 W. South Boulder Rd., Ste. 1
Louisville, CO 80027-1130
Phone: (800) 225-6482
Email: permissions@nita.org

ISBN 979-8-88669-019-4
FBA 2019
eISBN 979-8-88669-020-0
eFBA 2020

Printed in the United States of America

ASPEN PUBLISHING

Official co-publisher of NITA.
aspenpublishing.com/NITA

Contents

Case Synopsis

This case arises out of an automobile-pedestrian incident that occurred at approximately 6:00 p.m. on September 4, YR-2, at the corner of Broadway and Washington in Nita City. The plaintiff, Taylor Chen, was walking in a crosswalk when struck by a car driven by defendant and KarPül driver, Alex Miller. Chen has brought a negligence action for personal injury damages against Miller.

Alex Miller was on the way to pick up a KarPül rideshare rider at the time of the incident. Chen alleges that Miller was negligent and did not drive as a reasonably careful person would drive under the circumstances. Chen alleges that Miller drove negligently into a crosswalk, running a red light and striking Chen, causing severe injuries.

Miller denies negligence. Miller claims that the intersection was properly entered on a yellow light. Defendant alleges that Chen was 100 percent comparatively negligent when crossing negligently in front of the car while not looking for traffic and using a cell phone. Therefore, Miller is not liable for negligence.

At the time of the incident, Chen was an importer and exporter of textiles for one of the largest fashion design companies in the United States, earning an annual salary of $350,000. Chen has resigned from this job and claims an inability to work because of the injuries sustained in this incident.

INSTRUCTIONS FOR USE

Witnesses: The following witnesses are available for examination.

Plaintiff

Taylor Chen (Plaintiff)
Max O'Brien, NuNu Nectarine Chief Buyer
Evan Campbell, Treating and Expert Neurologist

Defendant

Alex Miller (Defendant)
Jesse Smith, Eye Witness and KarPül Rider
Quinn Cameron, Expert Neurologist

Stipulations:

Formula for Calculating Speed: The parties stipulate that the formula for calculating the feet per second a vehicle travels is: miles per hour × 1.47 = feet per second.

"All-Red Time" in Nita: The time from when a red light is displayed and when a cross street is given a green light is called the "All-Red Time." In Nita, the All-Red Time is 2.5 seconds. This allows cars to clear the intersection without causing a collision.

Exhibits and Documents: Exhibits and documents are all authentic and it can be assumed that witness testimony will lay required foundation.

Damages:

This case can be argued with or without the amount of damages at issue. The case can be bifurcated with only liability decided or the amount of damages can be argued by participants. Alternative instructions will be noted.

If participants will argue damages, the following stipulations should apply:

- Taylor Chen was earning $350,000 at the time of the incident.
- The standard work-life expectancy (age of retirement) is 67 years old.
- Taylor Chen's life expectancy is 82 years old.
- Taylor Chen's actual medical costs to date are: $90,000
- Taylor Chen claims that future medical costs are $50,000.

Years:

All years in these materials are stated in the following form:

1) YR-0 indicates the actual year in which the case is being tried (i.e., the present year);

2) YR-1 indicates the next preceding year (please use the actual year);

3) YR-2 indicates the second preceding year (please use the actual year), etc.

Color copies of the exhibits are available online at:

http://bit.ly/1P20Jea
Password: Chen1

PLEADINGS

B. Anita, NA SBN 16453
ANITA & ASSOCIATES, LLP
6490 Cascade Street, Suite 105
Nita City, Nita 12345
Tel.: (555) 235-6878
E-mail: banita@anitalaw.com

Attorneys for Plaintiff

SUPERIOR COURT OF THE STATE OF NITA
COUNTY OF NITA CITY

37–YR-0–00024369–CU–BT–CTL

Taylor Chen,	)	Case No.
	)	
Plaintiff,	)	COMPLAINT FOR NEGLIGENCE
	)	
v.	)	No. CV-235894
	)	
Alex Miller,	)	
	)	
Defendant.	)	

Plaintiff Taylor Chen for the complaint against Defendant Alex Miller states and alleges as follows:

I.

At all times relevant to this action Plaintiff Taylor Chen has been and is a resident of the County of Nita City, State of Nita and currently resides at 1015 Silver Stream Road, Nita City, Nita.

II.

At all times relevant to this action Defendant Alex Miller has been and is a resident of the County of Nita City, State of Nita and currently resides at 6262 Fox Hunt Street, Nita City, Nita.

III.

On or about September 4, YR-2, at approximately 6:00 p.m., Defendant Alex Miller, a KarPül rideshare driver, was operating a vehicle travelling Westbound on Washington Street, near Broadway, in Nita City, Nita.

IV.

Plaintiff Taylor Chen, a pedestrian, was waiting on the northwest corner of Broadway and Washington Street to cross over Washington Street in a southbound direction. When the walk signal turned green, Plaintiff Chen began to cross the street in a designated crosswalk.

V.

Defendant negligently proceeded through the intersection on a red light and struck Plaintiff Taylor Chen.

VI.

As a direct result of Defendant's negligence, Plaintiff has suffered numerous injuries. Because of these injuries, Plaintiff has incurred past medical expenses, including hospital and emergency care, and continues to require future medical care, thereby incurring future medical expenses.

VII.

As a direct result of Defendant's negligence, Plaintiff has in the past and will in the future suffer a loss of earnings and loss of earning capacity.

VIII.

As a direct result of Defendant's negligence, Plaintiff has in the past and will in the future suffer emotional distress, pain and suffering, and loss of enjoyment of life.

CLAIM 1: NEGLIGENCE

IX.

Defendant Miller acted negligently when driving and in a manner that placed Plaintiff and other pedestrians in danger, subsequently striking Plaintiff with the vehicle Defendant Miller was operating.

X.

Defendant Miller's negligent behavior in driving the vehicle was the direct cause of Plaintiff's severe and numerous injuries and damages.

XI.

As a direct result of Defendant Miller's carelessness and negligence, Plaintiff has incurred, and will incur in the future, economic damages including medical expenses and loss of earnings and non-economic damages including emotional distress, pain and suffering, and loss of enjoyment of life.

WHEREFORE Plaintiff prays for the following relief:

1) Awarding Plaintiff the past medical expenses in an amount to be determined.

2) Awarding Plaintiff all future medical expenses in an amount to be determined.

3) Awarding Plaintiff compensation for loss of earnings in an amount to be determined.

4) Awarding Plaintiff compensation for future lost earning capacity in an amount to be determined.

5) Awarding Plaintiff compensation for non-economic damages including for emotional distress, pain and suffering, and loss of enjoyment of life.

6) Awarding Plaintiff any and all other remedies the court so deems just.

Date: July 2, YR-1

B. Anita

B. Anita
ATTORNEY FOR PLAINTIFF

C. Harris, NA SBN 28105
HARRIS, MATHERS & ROSS, LLP
1600 Janan Place, Suite 200
Nita City, Nita 12345
Tel.: (555) 547-7500
E-mail: charris@HMR.com

Attorneys for Defendant

SUPERIOR COURT OF THE STATE OF NITA
COUNTY OF NITA CITY

Taylor Chen,	)	Case No. 37–YR-0–00024369–CU–BT–CTL
	)	
Plaintiff,	)	Dept.: 8
	)	Judge: C. Under
v.	)	
	)	
Alex Miller,	)	Complaint Filed: July 2, YR-1
	)	Trial Date: December 15, YR-0
Defendant.	)	

ANSWER

The Defendant states the following as Answer to Plaintiff's complaint:

1) Admits each and every allegation in paragraphs I through III.

2) In answer to the allegations in paragraphs IV through XI, Defendant is informed and believes that the allegations are untrue; and based on that information and belief denies the truth of each and every allegation in the paragraphs.

FIRST AFFIRMATIVE DEFENSE: COMPARATIVE FAULT

As a first affirmative defense, Defendant alleges Plaintiff was guilty of comparative fault in that Plaintiff as a pedestrian failed to keep a proper lookout for automobiles on the roadway and, instead, rushed out from the sidewalk directly into the path of Defendant's car. Plaintiff failed to exercise ordinary care on Plaintiff's own behalf with regard to the incident alleged in Plaintiff's complaint in the following respects:

1) Plaintiff failed to keep an adequate lookout for vehicles using the roadway;
2) Plaintiff failed to cross on a green light; and
3) Plaintiff failed to undertake proper acts to avoid or evade the claimed injury.

The preceding acts or omissions of Plaintiff were negligent, and Plaintiff's negligence caused and/or contributed to the damages complained of in this case. Accordingly, Plaintiff's damages should be proportionately reduced by an amount commensurate with Plaintiff's own negligence.

SECOND AFFIRMATIVE DEFENSE: ASSUMPTION OF THE RISK

As a second affirmative defense, Defendant alleges that Plaintiff attempted to cross the street at Broadway and Washington at a time and in a manner that was unsafe. Plaintiff rushed out from the sidewalk directly into the path of Defendant's car while Defendant had the green light. Plaintiff knew of this risk and voluntarily undertook the risk that led to the accident and the injuries complained of in this case.

THIRD AFFIRMATIVE DEFENSE: INEVITABLE ACCIDENT

As a third affirmative defense, Defendant alleges that if Plaintiff was not guilty of comparative fault that directly and proximately caused the injury, then the injury directly and proximately resulted from an unavoidable accident, in that Defendant driver did not and could not, by the exercise of ordinary care, see Plaintiff or anticipate Plaintiff's presence or position in the street as alleged by Plaintiff.
Defendant asks the Court that:

1) Plaintiff's complaint be dismissed with prejudice and that Plaintiff take nothing;
2) Defendant be awarded the costs of this action; and
3) Defendant be granted such other and further relief as the court deems proper.

Date: July 19, YR-1

C. Harris

C. Harris
ATTORNEY FOR DEFENDANT

SUPERIOR COURT OF THE STATE OF NITA
COUNTY OF NITA CITY

Taylor Chen,	)	Case No. 37–YR-0–00024369–CU–BT–CTL
	)	
Plaintiff,	)	**JOINT STATEMENT OF THE CASE**
	)	
v.	)	Dept.: 8
	)	Judge: C. Under
Alex Miller,	)	
	)	Complaint Filed: July 2, YR-1
Defendant.	)	Trial Date: December 15, YR-0

1) All parties have joined in the filing of this Joint Statement of the Case.
2) Estimated trial time: 1 day.
3) Jury is requested by the: Plaintiff.
4) Concise statement of the case including facts plaintiff(s) intend to prove, facts defendant(s) intend to prove, and legal basis for claims:

On September 4, YR-2, at approximately 6:00 p.m., KarPül rideshare driver Alex Miller responded to a pick-up request in Nita City. On his way to pick up his rider, Miller drove west on Washington Street. As Miller proceeded through the intersection of Broadway and Washington Street, Miller's car struck Taylor Chen, who was crossing the street in a marked crosswalk. Police and paramedics were called to the scene. The attending officer did not issue any traffic citation to Alex Miller. Chen was transported to the hospital with a hip and head injury.

Plaintiff Chen intends to prove that Miller negligently drove and struck Chen, resulting in severe damage to Chen. Specifically, Chen intends to prove that Miller was distracted while driving and drove negligently into a crosswalk, running a red light and striking Chen, causing injuries.

Defendant Alex Miller denies negligence. Miller claims to have properly entered the intersection on a yellow light. Miller alleges that Chen was negligent when entering the intersection and did not take proper care. Miller claims that Chen was using a cell phone instead of watching for traffic and negligently stepped into the road without a green walk signal. Miller intends to prove that Chen's negligence was the cause of the incident and that Miller is not liable.

5) The following are facts and issues that remain disputed among the Defendant and Plaintiff.

The parties dispute whether Chen or Miller had the right-of-way. The parties dispute who is responsible for the accident. The parties dispute whether Chen or Miller were negligent. The parties dispute the extent of Chen's damages.

6) List the names and addresses of witnesses that either party may call. Indicate the party who expects to call the witness and whether the party intends to qualify that witness as an expert.

Party	Name of Witness	Please Indicate If Expert Witness
Plaintiff	Taylor Chen	Lay Witness
Plaintiff	Max O'Brien	Lay Witness
Plaintiff	Evan Campbell	Expert Witness
Defendant	Alex Miller	Lay Witness
Defendant	Jesse Smith	Lay Witness
Defendant	Quinn Cameron	Expert Witness

7) The parties agree as to the preliminary and final jury instructions.

The undersigned counsel have met and conferred this September 8, YR-0 and certify the foregoing is true and correct.

B. Anita
B. Anita
ATTORNEY FOR PLAINTIFF

C. Harris
C. Harris
ATTORNEY FOR DEFENDANT

B. Anita, NA SBN 16453
ANITA & ASSOCIATES, LLP
6490 Cascade Street, Suite 105
Nita City, Nita 12345
Tel.: (555) 235-6878
E-mail: banita@anitalaw.com

Attorneys for PLAINTIFF

SUPERIOR COURT OF THE STATE OF NITA
COUNTY OF NITA CITY

Taylor Chen, Plaintiff, v. Alex Miller, Defendant.	Case No. 37–YR-0–00024369–CU–BT–CTL **PLAINTIFF'S RESPONSES TO FORM INTERROGATORIES, SET ONE** Dept.: 8 Judge: C. Under Complaint Filed: July 2, YR-1 Trial Date: December 15, YR-0

PROPOUNDING PARTY: Defendant Alex Miller
RESPONDING PARTY: Plaintiff Taylor Chen
SET NO.: One

(EXCERPTED) RESPONSES TO FORM INTERROGATORIES

<u>INTERROGATORY NO. 1.1:</u>

State the name, **ADDRESS**, telephone number, and relationship to you of each **PERSON** who prepared or assisted in the preparation of the responses to these interrogatories. (*Do not identify anyone who simply typed or reproduced the responses.*)

<u>RESPONSE:</u>

Taylor Chen, plaintiff, can be contacted through counsel.
Ryan Chen, spouse, can be contacted through counsel.
B. Anita, attorney.

INTERROGATORY NO. 2.1:

State:
(a) your name;
(b) every name you have used in the past; and
(c) the dates you used each name

RESPONSE:

(a) Taylor Chen;
(b) Taylor McGuiness (name prior to marriage);
(c) Married in YR-13.

INTERROGATORY NO. 2.2:

State the date and place of your birth.

RESPONSE:

November 6, YR-50; Nita City, Nita.

...

INTERROGATORY NO. 2.5:

State:
(a) your present residence **ADDRESS**;
(b) your residence **ADDRESSES** for the past five years; and
(c) the dates you lived at each **ADDRESS**.

RESPONSE:

(a) 1014 Silver Stream Road, Nita City, Nita;
(b) SAME;
(c) N/A.

INTERROGATORY NO. 2.6:

State:
(a) the name, **ADDRESS**, and telephone number of your present employer or place of self-employment; and
(b) the name, **ADDRESS**, dates of employment, job title, and nature of work for each employer or self-employment you have had from five years before the **INCIDENT** until today.

RESPONSE:

(a) Currently unemployed, however, earn some income writing a blog and through speaking engagements.
(b) NuNu Nectarine, 700 First Street, Nita City, Nita, buyer on import/export team, Dates of Employment: YR-14 through February, YR-1.

INTERROGATORY NO. 2.7:

State:
(a) the name and **ADDRESS** of each school or other academic or vocational institution you have attended, beginning with high school;
(b) the dates you attended;
(c) the highest grade level you have completed; and
(d) the degrees received.

RESPONSE:

(a) Nita City High School; University of Nita; Nita State University;
(b) graduated in YR-32; graduated in YR-28; graduated in YR-24;
(c) completed all years of each institution;
(d) High school diploma; BS in business and communications from University of Nita; Master's in business administration from Nita State University.

INTERROGATORY NO. 2.8:

Have you ever been convicted of a felony?

RESPONSE:

No.

INTERROGATORY NO. 2.9:

Can you speak English with ease? If not, what language and dialect do you normally use?

RESPONSE:

Yes.

. . .

INTERROGATORY NO. 2.12:

At the time of the **INCIDENT** did you or any other person have any physical, emotional, or mental disability or condition that may have contributed to the occurrence of the **INCIDENT**?

RESPONSE:

At the time of the accident, I did not have any physical, emotional, or mental disability or condition that contributed to the accident. I am unaware as to whether any other person had any physical, emotional, or mental disability or condition that may have contributed to the accident.

INTERROGATORY NO. 2.13:

Within 24 hours before the **INCIDENT** did you or any person involved in the **INCIDENT** use or take any of the following substances: alcoholic beverage, marijuana, or other drug or medication of any kind (prescription or other)?

RESPONSE:

Within twenty-four hours before the accident, I did not use or take any of the listed substances. I am unaware as to whether the defendant, Alex Miller, used any of the listed substances.

. . .

INTERROGATORY NO. 6.1:

Do you attribute any physical, mental, or emotional injuries to the **INCIDENT**?

RESPONSE:

Yes.

INTERROGATORY NO. 6.2:

Identify each injury you attribute to the **INCIDENT** and the area of your body affected.

RESPONSE:

Contusion of the head, severe concussion, knee strain injury, broken pelvis, leg hematoma, bruising, migraines; anxiety regarding future brain complications, early onset dementia, early arthritis.

INTERROGATORY NO. 6.3:

Do you still have any complaints that you attribute to the **INCIDENT**? If so, for each complaint state:
(a) a description
(b) whether the complaint is subsiding, remaining the same, or becoming worse; and
(c) the frequency and duration.

RESPONSE:

Yes.
(a) Some soreness in hip, migraines about once a month, anxiety, worry and concern about
future complications relating to accident;
(b) Subsiding or remaining the same;
(c) Daily.

INTERROGATORY NO. 6.4:

Did you receive any consultation or examination or treatment from a **HEALTH CARE PROVIDER** for any injury you attribute to the **INCIDENT**? If so, for each **HEALTH CARE PROVIDER** state:
(a) the name, **ADDRESS**, and telephone number;
(b) the type of consultation, examination, or treatment provided
(c) the dates you received consultation, examination, or treatment; and
(d) the charges to date.

RESPONSE:

Yes.
(a) General Hospital: emergency room and trauma center;
(b) Emergency medical services; trauma center; CT scan, X-rays; stitches for head contusion; physical therapy for knee and hip injuries; visits to neurologist for migraines in follow-up to accident.
(c) Majority of the treatment was received in the fourteen days following the accident; I had follow-up physical therapy twice a week for several weeks after my discharge; follow-up with my neurologist for migraines since the accident.
(d) $80,000.

INTERROGATORY NO. 6.5:

Have you taken any medication, prescribed or not, as a result of injuries that you attribute to the **INCIDENT**? If so, for each medication state:

(a) the name;
(b) the **PERSON** who prescribed or furnished it;
(c) the date it was prescribed or furnished;
(d) the dates you began and stopped taking it; and
(e) the cost to date.

RESPONSE:

Yes.
(a) Painkillers following accident; migraine medication; over-the-counter pain medicine;
(b) Evan Campbell, M.D.
(c) On the date of the accident.
(d) Continuing as needed for migraines and pain.
(e) $5,000.

. . .

INTERROGATORY NO. 6.7:

Has any **HEALTH CARE PROVIDER** advised that you may require future or additional treatment for any injuries that you attribute to the **INCIDENT**? If so, for each injury state:
(a) the name and **ADDRESS** of each **HEALTH CARE PROVIDER**;
(b) the complaints for which the treatment was advised; and
(c) the nature, duration, and estimated cost of the treatment.

RESPONSE:

Yes.
(a) Evan Campbell, M.D.
(b) Migraines, possible early onset dementia; possible early onset arthritis;
(c) Migraine medication and other treatment, to continue as needed and indefinitely at an estimated cost of $50,000.

INTERROGATORY NO. 7.1:

Do you attribute any loss of or damage to a vehicle or other property to the **INCIDENT**?

RESPONSE:

NONE.
. . .

INTERROGATORY NO. 8.1:

Do you attribute any loss of income or earning capacity to the **INCIDENT**? (*If your answer is "no," do not answer interrogatories 8.2 through 8.8.*)

RESPONSE:

Yes.

INTERROGATORY NO. 8.2:

State:
(a) the nature of your work;
(b) your job title at the time of the **INCIDENT**; and
(c) the date your employment began.

RESPONSE:

(a) Buyer on import/export team with NuNu Nectarine;
(b) Buyer on import/export team with NuNu Nectarine;
(c) YR-13.

INTERROGATORY NO. 8.3:

State the last date before the **INCIDENT** that you worked for compensation.

RESPONSE:

September 4, YR-2.

INTERROGATORY NO. 8.4:

State your monthly income at the time of the **INCIDENT** and how the amount was calculated.

RESPONSE:

$29,166 per month based on a yearly salary of $350,000.

INTERROGATORY NO. 8.5:

State the date you returned to work at each place of employment following the **INCIDENT**.

RESPONSE:

I never returned to work on a full-time basis but engaged in part-time work beginning in November, YR-2.

INTERROGATORY NO. 8.6:

State the dates you did not work and for which you lost income as a result of the **INCIDENT**.

RESPONSE:

I officially resigned from my employment with NuNu Nectarine in February YR-1.

INTERROGATORY NO. 8.7:

State the total income you have lost to date as a result of the **INCIDENT** and how the amount was calculated.

RESPONSE:

$350,000 per year since February YR-1.

INTERROGATORY NO. 8.8:

Will you lose income in the future as a result of the **INCIDENT**? If so, state:
(a) the facts upon which you base this contention;
(b) an estimate of the amount;
(c) an estimate of how long you will be unable to work; and
(d) how the claim for future income is calculated.

RESPONSE:

Yes.
(a) I resigned from my position at NuNu Nectarine in February YR-1 because I could no longer perform my job;
(b) Between $6.6 million and $17 million; I will lose at least $350,000 per year until the age of my retirement (67), this is $6.6 million; I was being considered for a promotion prior to the accident which would have eventually increased my yearly salary to over $1 million, and therefore the potential for my future lost income is close to $17 million;
(c) I do not believe I will ever be able to work again in this capacity;
(d) I calculated my future income by multiplying my yearly income by my years left until retirement.

INTERROGATORY NO. 9.1:

Are there any other damages that you attribute to the **INCIDENT**? If so, for each item of damage state:
(a) the nature;
(b) the date it occurred;
(c) the amount; and
(d) the name, **ADDRESS**, and telephone number of each **PERSON** to whom an obligation was incurred.

RESPONSE:

Yes.
(a) I worry about having future physical complications and neurological complications from the injuries I sustained in the accident;
(b) Daily since the accident;
(c) N/A;
(d) N/A.

. . .

INTERROGATORY NO. 10.1:

At any time before the **INCIDENT** did you have complaints or injuries that involved the same part of your body claimed to have been injured in the **INCIDENT**?

RESPONSE:

NONE.

INTERROGATORY NO. 10.2:

List all physical, mental, and emotional disabilities you had immediately before the **INCIDENT**. (*You may omit mental or emotional disabilities unless you attribute any mental or emotional injury to the INCIDENT.*)

RESPONSE:

NONE.

INTERROGATORY NO. 10.3:

At any time after the **INCIDENT**, did you sustain injuries of the kind for which you are now claiming damages?

RESPONSE:

NONE.

INTERROGATORY NO. 11.1:

Except for this action, in the past ten years have you filed an action or made a written claim or demand for compensation for your personal injuries?

RESPONSE:

NONE.

INTERROGATORY NO. 11.2:

In the past ten years have you made a written claim or demand for workers' compensation benefits?

RESPONSE:

NONE.

. . .

INTERROGATORY NO. 12.1:

State the name, **ADDRESS**, and telephone number of each individual:

(a) who witnessed the **INCIDENT** or the events occurring immediately before or after the **INCIDENT**;

(b) who made any statement at the scene of the **INCIDENT**;

(c) who heard any statements made about the **INCIDENT** by any individual at the scene; and

(d) who **YOU OR ANYONE ACTING ON YOUR BEHALF** claim has knowledge of the **INCIDENT** (except for expert witnesses covered by Code of Civil Procedure section 2034).

RESPONSE:

All of my information comes from the police report for this accident.

INTERROGATORY NO. 12.2:

Have **YOU OR ANYONE ACTING ON YOUR BEHALF** interviewed any individual concerning the **INCIDENT**?

RESPONSE:

All of my information comes from the police report for this accident.

. . .

INTERROGATORY NO. 14.1:

Do **YOU OR ANYONE ACTING ON YOUR BEHALF** contend that any **PERSON** involved in the **INCIDENT** violated any statute, ordinance, or regulation and that the violation was a legal (proximate) cause of the **INCIDENT**? If so, identify the name, **ADDRESS**, and telephone number of each **PERSON** and the statute, ordinance, or regulation that was violated.

RESPONSE:

I contend that the defendant, Alex Miller, may have violated Nita Traffic Statutes pertaining to the safe operation of a vehicle. NRC 45-13-02

INTERROGATORY NO. 14.2:

Was any **PERSON** cited or charged with a violation of any statute, ordinance, or regulation as a result of this **INCIDENT**?

RESPONSE:

NONE.

. . .

INTERROGATORY NO. 20.1:

State the date, time, and place of the **INCIDENT** (closest street **ADDRESS** or intersection).

RESPONSE:

September 4, YR-1; 6:00 p.m.; Washington Street and Broadway intersection.

INTERROGATORY NO. 20.2:

For each vehicle involved in the **INCIDENT**, state:
(a) the year, make, model, and license number;
(b) the name, **ADDRESS**, and telephone number of the driver;
(c) the name, **ADDRESS**, and telephone number of each occupant other than the driver;
(d) the name, **ADDRESS**, and telephone number of each registered owner;

(e) the name, **ADDRESS**, and telephone number of each lessee;
(f) the name, **ADDRESS**, and telephone number of each owner other than the registered owner or lien holder; and
(g) the name of each owner who gave permission or consent to the driver to operate the vehicle.

RESPONSE:

(a) YR-6 Toyota Camry, License number PKU 444;
(b) Alex Miller;
(c) NONE;
(d) Do not know;
(e) NONE;
(f) NONE;
(g) Do not know, possibly KarPül.

INTERROGATORY NO. 20.3:

State the **ADDRESS** and location where your trip began and the **ADDRESS** and location of your destination.

RESPONSE:

I began walking from my job at NuNu Nectarine, I stopped at Party Central on Broadway to purchase a bunch of balloons. I was walking towards my home at the time of the accident.

INTERROGATORY NO. 20.4:

Describe the route that you followed from the beginning of your trip to the location of the **INCIDENT**, and state the location of each stop, other than routine traffic stops, during the trip leading up to the **INCIDENT**.

RESPONSE:

I began walking from my job at NuNu Nectarine, I stopped at Party Central on Broadway to purchase a bunch of balloons. I was walking towards my home at the time of the accident. Right before I was hit, I was walking south on the west sidewalk of Broadway. I was waiting at the corner of Broadway and Washington Street for the walk light to turn green so that I could cross from the north to the south on the west side of Broadway. As the signal came on, I started walking across the street. I had taken about two steps when the car hit me.

INTERROGATORY NO. 20.5:

State the name of the street or roadway, the lane of travel, and the direction of travel of each vehicle involved in the **INCIDENT** for the 500 feet of travel before the **INCIDENT**.

RESPONSE:

The car that hit me was driving on Washington Street from my left to my right (east to west) going through the Broadway intersection.

INTERROGATORY NO. 20.6:

Did the **INCIDENT** occur at an intersection? If so, describe all traffic control devices, signals, or signs at the intersection.

RESPONSE:

The accident occurred at the intersection of Broadway and Washington Street. Washington Street runs east to west and Broadway runs north to south. There are traffic signals on all four corners of the intersection. I could clearly see the walk signal and the light for my crossing on Broadway across Washington Street. I saw the light for my direction of travel change from red to green. I also saw the pedestrian signal change from the red hand (stop signal) to the green walker (walk signal). There was also a traffic signal for traffic going east to west.

INTERROGATORY NO. 20.7:

Was there a traffic signal facing you at the time of the **INCIDENT**? If so, state:
(a) your location when you first saw it;
(b) the color;
(c) the number of seconds it had been that color; and
(d) whether the color changed between the time you first saw it and the **INCIDENT**.

RESPONSE:

Yes.
(a) I saw the traffic signal as I was walking on Broadway going south before I crossed Washington Street;
(b) It was red for me when I first saw it;
(c) I do not know, I probably saw it for three seconds;
(d) I remember the walk signal and light turning green. As the walk signal came on and the light turned green, I started crossing the street and was soon hit by the car.

INTERROGATORY NO. 20.8:

State how the **INCIDENT** occurred, giving the speed, direction, and location of each vehicle involved:
(a) just before the **INCIDENT**;
(b) at the time of the **INCIDENT**; and
(c) just after the **INCIDENT**.

RESPONSE:

As the light turned green and the walk signal came on, I crossed south on Broadway across Washington Street. I had taken two steps, approximately six feet total, when the car seemed to come out of nowhere and hit me. I was only aware of the car right before I was hit. It was traveling from my left to my right (East to West) on Washington Street. After the accident, I think that I lost consciousness. I do not remember actually being hit, flying through the air, or falling; I do not remember anything for several minutes of time. The first thing I remember seeing is the car coming to a stop and the driver approaching to check on me.

INTERROGATORY NO. 20.9:

Do you have information that a malfunction or defect in a vehicle caused the **INCIDENT**?

RESPONSE:

NONE.

INTERROGATORY NO. 20.10:

Do you have information that any malfunction or defect in a vehicle contributed to the injuries sustained in the **INCIDENT**?

RESPONSE:

NONE.
Dated: September 1, YR-1

Anita & Associate.s
By: B. Anita
B. Anita
Attorney for Plaintiff Taylor Chen

C. Harris, NA SBN 28105
HARRIS, MATHERS & ROSS, LLP
1600 Janan Place, Suite 200
Nita City, Nita 12345
Tel.: (555) 547-7500
E-mail: charris@HMR.com

Attorneys for DEFENDANT

SUPERIOR COURT OF THE STATE OF NITA
COUNTY OF NITA CITY

Taylor Chen,	)	Case No. 37–YR-0–00024369–CU–BT–CTL
	)	
Plaintiff,	)	**DEFENDANT'S RESPONSES TO FORM INTERROGATORIES, SET ONE**
	)	
v.	)	
	)	Dept.: 8
Alex Miller,	)	Judge: C. Under
	)	
	)	Complaint Filed: July 2, YR-1
Defendants.	)	Trial Date: December 15, YR-0

PROPOUNDING PARTY: Plaintiff Taylor Chen
RESPONDING PARTY: Defendant Alex Miller
SET NO.: One

(EXCERPTED) RESPONSES TO FORM INTERROGATORIES

RESPONSE TO FORM INTERROGATORY NO. 1.1:

Alex Miller, defendant, can be contacted through counsel, C. Harris.
Robert Ramirez, attorney for KarPül, can be contacted through counsel.

RESPONSE TO FORM INTERROGATORY NO. 2.1:

(a) Alexander Miller;
(b) Alex Miller and Alexander Miller, interchangeably;
(c) N/A.

RESPONSE TO FORM INTERROGATORY NO. 2.2:

July 15, YR-31; Boulder, Colorado.

RESPONSE TO FORM INTERROGATORY NO. 2.3:

Yes.

(a) Nita;
(b) M-878021662323 general type;
(c) 2007;
(d) NONE.
. . .

RESPONSE TO FORM INTERROGATORY NO. 2.5:

(a) 6262 Fox Hunt Street, Nita City, Nita;
(b) Same;
(c) N/A.

RESPONSE TO FORM INTERROGATORY NO. 2.6:

(a) Coffee Cup, Nita City, Nita; (341) 123-4567; employed since YR-6;
(b) KarPül Rideshare, Nita City, Nita; (800) 987-6543; driving since YR-2.

RESPONSE TO FORM INTERROGATORY NO. 2.7:

(a) Boulder High School;
(b) Graduated Boulder High School in YR-13;
(c) 12;
(d) High school diploma.

RESPONSE TO FORM INTERROGATORY NO. 2.8:

NONE.

RESPONSE TO FORM INTERROGATORY NO. 2.9:

Yes.
. . .

RESPONSE TO FORM INTERROGATORY NO. 2.11:

No, at the time of the incident I was working as an independent contractor driving for KarPül.

<u>RESPONSE TO FORM INTERROGATORY NO. 2.12:</u>

NONE.

<u>RESPONSE TO FORM INTERROGATORY NO. 2.13:</u>

NONE.

. . .

<u>RESPONSE TO FORM INTERROGATORY NO. 6.1:</u>

NONE.

. . .

<u>RESPONSE TO FORM INTERROGATORY NO. 8.1:</u>

NONE.

<u>RESPONSE TO FORM INTERROGATORY NO. 9.1:</u>

NONE.

. . .

<u>RESPONSE TO FORM INTERROGATORY NO. 12.1:</u>

The only information that I have in response to this interrogatory is contained in the police report for this incident.

<u>RESPONSE TO FORM INTERROGATORY NO. 12.2:</u>

The only information that I have in response to this interrogatory is contained in the police report for this incident.

<u>RESPONSE TO FORM INTERROGATORY NO. 12.3:</u>

The only information that I have in response to this interrogatory is contained in the police report for this incident.

. . .

<u>RESPONSE TO FORM INTERROGATORY NO. 12.5:</u>

The only information that I have in response to this interrogatory is contained in the police report for this incident.

RESPONSE TO FORM INTERROGATORY NO. 12.6:

The only information that I have in response to this interrogatory is contained in the police report for this incident.

. . .

RESPONSE TO FORM INTERROGATORY NO. 14.1:

Plaintiff Taylor Chen may have violated Nita Traffic Statutes regarding safe traffic practices for a pedestrian. NRC 45-11-46.

RESPONSE TO FORM INTERROGATORY NO. 14.2:

NONE.

RESPONSE TO FORM INTERROGATORY NO. 15.1:

(a) I was not careless or negligent and I did not cause this incident. I was not intoxicated. I was driving very carefully at the time of the accident, even under the speed limit because it was a busy evening and there were lots of cars and pedestrians around. I was not in a hurry. The light was green for me on Washington as I approached the intersection with Broadway. I was driving towards the west. At that time, I started going even slower. The light turned yellow when I got to the intersection, and I did not speed up to get through it. After I crossed the intersection, the plaintiff suddenly stepped off the curb right in front of my car. I could not stop in time to avoid hitting the pedestrian. The plaintiff failed to watch for cars in the roadway and tried to cross the street at a time that was unsafe. The plaintiff rushed out from the sidewalk directly in the path of my car.

(b) Myself and maybe other eyewitnesses mentioned in the police report;

(c) Nita City Police Report, Case No. 9999-0000.

RESPONSE TO FORM INTERROGATORY NO. 16.1:

NONE.

RESPONSE TO FORM INTERROGATORY NO. 16.2:

I do not have any information about the extent of the plaintiff's injuries. The car was not damaged at all. I do not think it hit hard, just bumped. My actions in the incident did not cause any injuries; instead, the plaintiff's own carelessness and negligence caused the injuries.

RESPONSE TO FORM INTERROGATORY NO. 16.3:

I do not have any information about the extent of the plaintiff's injuries. The car was not damaged at all. I do not think it hit her hard, just bumped her. My actions in the incident did not cause any injuries; instead, the plaintiff's own carelessness and negligence caused the injuries.

RESPONSE TO FORM INTERROGATORY NO. 16.4:

I do not have any information about the extent of the plaintiff's injuries. The car was not damaged at all. I do not think it hit anyone hard, just bumped. My actions in the incident did not cause any injuries; instead, the plaintiff's own carelessness and negligence caused the injuries.

. . .

RESPONSE TO FORM INTERROGATORY NO. 16.6:

I do not have any information about the extent of the plaintiff's injuries. The car was not damaged at all. I do not think it hit anyone hard, just bumped. My actions in the incident did not cause any injuries; instead, the plaintiff's own carelessness and negligence caused the injuries.

. . .

RESPONSE TO FORM INTERROGATORY NO. 20.1:

September 4, YR-1 at 6:00 p.m. The incident occurred at the corner of Washington Street and Broadway.

RESPONSE TO FORM INTERROGATORY NO. 20.2:

(a) YR-6, Toyota Camry, license number PKU 444;
(b) Alex Miller, can be contacted through counsel;
(c) NONE;
(d) Alex Miller and Kai Miller, can be contacted through counsel;
(e) NONE;
(f) NONE;
(g) Kai Miller, can be contacted through counsel.

RESPONSE TO FORM INTERROGATORY NO. 20.3:

I began driving from the northeast section of Nita City and I was driving west on Washington to pick up a rider at the Florence Hotel at 5677 Washington Street.

RESPONSE TO FORM INTERROGATORY NO. 20.4:

I don't remember the exact route I followed. I had been driving for KarPül for several hours before the incident. My previous rider was dropped off in the northeast section of Nita City at the Corner Bar around 5:30. I remained in that area waiting for a new request until about 5:45 when I got the KarPül pick up request from J. Smith. The request stated that he wanted to be picked up on West Washington Street, so I drove that direction first and then realized he wanted a pickup at the Florence Hotel, which is on Washington Street, not West Washington. I had to circle around and was driving on Washington Street in a westbound direction for about a half a mile when the incident occurred at the intersection of Washington and Broadway.

RESPONSE TO FORM INTERROGATORY NO. 20.5:

I was traveling west on Washington Street. I was in the right-hand lane. Washington Street is a one-way street running east to west, I was traveling towards the west. I had just crossed through the Broadway intersection prior to the incident.

RESPONSE TO FORM INTERROGATORY NO. 20.6:

Yes. The incident occurred at the corner of Broadway and Washington. There were traffic signals on all four corners of the intersection. I could see the traffic signal on Washington Street at the corner of Broadway. The light was green for me as I approached Broadway. When I got to the intersection, the light turned yellow and it was yellow as I crossed the intersection. There was also a traffic signal and walk signal for the north/south direction on Broadway.

RESPONSE TO FORM INTERROGATORY NO. 20.7:

Yes.

(a) I first saw the traffic signal as I was driving on Washington Street and approached Broadway;
(b) It was green;
(c) I don't know how many seconds it had been green;
(d) The color changed from green to yellow when I got to the intersection.

RESPONSE TO FORM INTERROGATORY NO. 20.8:

I was driving towards the west on Washington Street. I was driving very carefully because there were lots of cars and people around on the streets. I was driving at a speed of less than twenty miles per hour. I was not in a hurry. As I approached the traffic light at Broadway, I saw that the light was green. At that time I started driving even slower, about five to ten miles per hour. There were pedestrians and traffic waiting for the light to change. When I got to the intersection, the light turned yellow. I did not stop in the crosswalk on the east side of Broadway because I didn't want to block the intersection or the street. I did not speed up to get through the intersection. When I crossed the intersection, a person suddenly stepped off the curb right in front of my car. I could not avoid hitting this person and could not stop in time. It was very sudden, and they appeared out of nowhere. I was able to stop about ten feet beyond the crosswalk. The person got hit on the left side of the body by the right front fender of my car. I first saw the person about five feet in front of the car.

. . .

RESPONSE TO FORM INTERROGATORY NO. 20.11:

My car was not damaged. I have kept possession of the car and continue to use it.
Dated: September 18, YR-1

The Law Office of C. Harris

By: C. Harris

C. HARRIS
Attorneys for Defendant Alex Miller

Jury Instructions

Preliminary Jury Instructions (Prior to Evidence)

General/Introductory:

1) You have now been sworn as jurors in this case. I want to impress on you the seriousness and importance of serving on a jury. Trial by jury is a fundamental right in Nita. The parties have a right to a jury that is selected fairly, that comes to the case without bias, and that will attempt to reach a verdict based on the evidence presented.
2) It is important that you keep an open mind throughout this trial. Evidence can only be presented a piece at a time. Do not form or express an opinion about this case while the trial is going on. You must not decide on a verdict until after you have heard all the evidence and have discussed it thoroughly with your fellow jurors in your deliberations.
3) You are responsible for deciding what the facts are in this case. Do not let bias, sympathy, prejudice, or public opinion influence your verdict.
4) At the end of the trial, I will explain the law that you must follow to reach your verdict. You must follow the law as I explain it to you, even if you do not agree with the law.

Case Overview:

1) To assist you in your tasks as jurors, I will now explain how the trial will proceed. I will begin by identifying the parties to the case. Taylor Chen filed this lawsuit and is called a plaintiff. Taylor Chen seeks damages from Alex Miller, who is called a defendant.
2) Plaintiff Taylor Chen claims that the defendant was negligent. Defendant Alex Miller denies this claim. Defendant contends that Taylor Chen's own negligence caused the damages.
3) You must not consider whether any of the parties in this case has insurance. The presence or absence of insurance is totally irrelevant. You must decide this case based only on the law and the evidence.

Final Jury Instructions (After Evidence and Argument)

General/Introductory

1) You have now heard the evidence and the argument. It is now my duty to instruct you on the law. You have two main duties as jurors.
   a) The first one is to decide what the facts are from the evidence that you saw and heard here in court. Deciding what the facts are is your job, not mine, and nothing that I have said or done during this trial was meant to influence your decision about the facts in any way.
   b) Your second duty is to take the law that I give you, apply it to the facts, and decide if, under the appropriate burden of proof, the parties have established their claims or defenses. In other words, it is your duty to determine from the evidence what actually happened in this case, applying the law as I now explain it.
   c) Perform these duties fairly. Do not let bias, sympathy, or prejudice that you may feel toward one side or the other influence your decision in any way.
2) While you may consider only the evidence in the case in arriving at your verdict, you are permitted to draw such reasonable inferences from the testimony and exhibits you feel are justified in the light of your experience, reason, and common sense.
3) There are two types of evidence used in this trial, direct evidence and circumstantial (or indirect) evidence. You may use both types of evidence in reaching your verdict. Direct evidence is simply evidence which, if believed, directly proves a fact. Circumstantial evidence is evidence which, if believed, indirectly proves a fact. For example, if someone walked into the courtroom wearing a wet raincoat and carrying a wet umbrella, that would be circumstantial evidence from which you could reasonably find or conclude that it was raining. The law makes no distinction between the weight that you should give to either direct or circumstantial evidence. It is for you to decide how much weight to give any evidence.
4) In deciding what the facts are, you must decide what testimony you believe and what testimony you do not believe. You are the sole judges of the credibility of the witnesses. Credibility refers to whether a witness is worthy of belief: Was the witness truthful? Was the witness accurate? You may believe everything a witness says, or only part of it, or none of it.

Plaintiff's Claim against Defendant

Taylor Chen claims to have been harmed by Alex Miller's negligence. To establish this claim, Taylor Chen must prove all of the following:

a) That Alex Miller, as a driver, had a duty to drive with reasonable care;

b) That Alex Miller failed to drive with reasonable care;

c) That Taylor Chen was harmed; and

d) That Alex Miller's negligence was a substantial factor in causing Taylor Chen's harm.

Comparative Fault of Plaintiff

Alex Miller claims that Taylor Chen's own negligence contributed to the harm. To succeed on this claim, Alex Miller must prove all of the following:

a) That Taylor Chen, as a pedestrian, had a duty to act as a reasonably careful pedestrian;

b) That Taylor Chen failed to act as a reasonably careful pedestrian; and

c) That Taylor Chen's own negligence was a substantial factor in causing the alleged harm.

If Alex Miller proves the above, Taylor Chen's damages are reduced by your determination of the percentage of responsibility. I will calculate the actual reduction.

Burden of Proof

1) The parties must persuade you, by the evidence presented in court, that what they are required to prove is more likely to be true than not true. This is referred to as "the burden of proof."

2) After weighing all of the evidence, if you cannot decide whether something is more likely to be true than not true, you must conclude that the party did not prove it. You should consider all the evidence, no matter which party produced the evidence.

3) In this case, Plaintiff Taylor Chen bears the burden of proof on the negligence claim against Alex Miller. In turn, Defendant Alex Miller bears the burden of proof on the defense that Taylor Chen's own negligence caused the harm.

Negligence Defined

1) Negligence is the failure to use reasonable care to prevent harm to oneself or to others. A person can be negligent by acting or by failing to act. A person is negligent if that person does something that a reasonably careful person would not do in the same situation, or fails to do something that a reasonably careful person would do in the same situation. You must decide how a reasonably careful person would have acted in this situation.

2) A person must use reasonable care in driving a vehicle. Drivers must keep a lookout for pedestrians, obstacles, and other vehicles. They must also control the speed and movement of their vehicles. The failure to use reasonable care in driving a vehicle is negligence.

3) A driver of a vehicle must yield the right-of-way to a pedestrian who is crossing the roadway within any marked crosswalk. When approaching a pedestrian who is within a crosswalk, a driver must use reasonable care and must reduce the vehicle's speed or take any other action necessary to ensure the safety of the pedestrian.

4) Pedestrians must also use reasonable care for their own safety. Pedestrians may not suddenly leave a curb or other place of safety and walk or run into the path of a vehicle that is so close as to constitute an immediate hazard.

5) The failure of a pedestrian to exercise reasonable care does not relieve a driver of a vehicle from the duty of exercising reasonable care for the safety of any pedestrian within any marked crosswalk.

Damages [Include these instructions only if using as a damages case file. If case is bifurcated (liability and damages decided separately), exclude these instructions.]

1) If you decide that Taylor Chen has proved the claim against Alex Miller, you also must decide how much money will reasonably compensate Taylor Chen for the harm. This compensation is called "damages."
2) The amount of damages must include an award for each item of harm that was caused by Alex Miller's wrongful conduct, even if the particular harm could not have been anticipated.
3) Taylor Chen does not have to prove the exact amount of damages that will provide reasonable compensation for the harm. However, you must not speculate or guess in awarding damages.
4) The following are the specific items of damages claimed by Taylor Chen:
    a) Economic damages:
        i) Medical expenses, past and future, and
        ii) Lost earnings, past and future
    b) Noneconomic damages:
        i) Physical pain,
        ii) Mental suffering, and
        iii) Emotional distress

SUPERIOR COURT OF THE STATE OF NITA
COUNTY OF NITA CITY

Taylor Chen,	)	Case No. 37–YR-0–00024369–CU–BT–CTL
	)	
Plaintiff,	)	Dept.: 8
	)	Judge: C. Under
v.	)	
	)	
Alex Miller,	)	Complaint Filed: July 2, YR-1
	)	Trial Date: December 15, YR-0
Defendant.	)	

VERDICT FORM [WITHOUT DAMAGES]

We, the jury, answer the questions submitted to us as follows:

QUESTION NO. 1: Was the Defendant Alex Miller negligent?

ANSWER:_______________ (Yes or No)

If your answer to question 1 is yes, then answer question 2. If you answered no, stop here, answer no further questions.

QUESTION NO. 2: Was the Defendant's negligence a substantial factor in causing harm to the Plaintiff?

ANSWER: ______________ (Yes or No)

QUESTION NO. 3: Was the Plaintiff Taylor Chen negligent?

ANSWER: ______________ (Yes or No)

If your answer to question 3 is yes, then answer question 4. If you answered no, stop here, answer no further questions.

QUESTION NO. 4: Was the Plaintiff's negligence a substantial factor in causing the harm?

ANSWER: _____________ (Yes or No)

If your answer to question 4 is yes, then answer question 5. If you answered no, stop here, answer no further questions.

QUESTION NO. 5: What percentage of responsibility for Plaintiff's harm do you assign to:

______ Defendant Alex Miller ______%

______ Plaintiff Taylor Chen ______%

Total 100%

Signed: ______________________________ Foreperson

SUPERIOR COURT OF THE STATE OF NITA
COUNTY OF NITA CITY

Taylor Chen,	)	Case No. 37–YR-0–00024369–CU–BT–CTL
	)	
Plaintiff,	)	Dept.: 8
	)	Judge: C. Under
v.	)	
	)	
Alex Miller,	)	Complaint Filed: July 2, YR-1
	)	Trial Date: December 15, YR-0
Defendant.	)	

VERDICT FORM [WITH DAMAGES]

We, the jury, answer the questions submitted to us as follows:

QUESTION NO. 1: Was the Defendant Alex Miller negligent?

ANSWER:_______________ (Yes or No)

If your answer to question 1 is yes, then answer question 2. If you answered no, stop here, answer no further questions.

QUESTION NO. 2: Was the Defendant's negligence a substantial factor in causing harm to the Plaintiff?

ANSWER: ______________ (Yes or No)

If your answer to question 2 is yes, then answer question 3. If you answered no, stop here, answer no further questions.

QUESTION NO. 3: What is the Plaintiff's total amount of damages? Do not reduce the damages based on the fault, if any, of the Plaintiff.

$______________________________

QUESTION NO. 4: Was the Plaintiff Taylor Chen negligent?

ANSWER: ______________ (Yes or No)

If your answer to question 4 is yes, then answer question 5. If you answered no, stop here, answer no further questions.

QUESTION NO. 5: Was the Plaintiff's negligence a substantial factor in causing the harm?

ANSWER: _____________ (Yes or No)

If your answer to question 5 is yes, then answer question 6. If you answered no, stop here, answer no further questions.

QUESTION NO. 6: What percentage of responsibility for Plaintiff's harm do you assign to:

______ Defendant Alex Miller ______%

______ Plaintiff Taylor Chen ______%

Total 100%

Signed: ______________________________ Foreperson

Deposition Transcripts

Deposition Transcript—Taylor Chen
November 13, YR-1

My name is Taylor Chen. I am forty-nine years old and live with my partner, Ryan Chen, at 1015 Silver Stream Road in Nita City. I am currently a social media influencer, an ultra-marathon runner, and a stay-at-home parent to my three children, Sam, Ben, and Carlie. My children range in ages from five to ten. My partner is an elementary school teacher.

I was born and raised here in Nita City, Nita. I graduated from Nita City High School in YR-32, where I ran track. I was named "most likely to succeed" by my graduating class and I truly felt that I was on the road to taking over the corporate world. I hadn't yet focused in on fashion, but I knew without a doubt that I wanted to be a businessperson, running an influential company. I received my undergraduate degree in business from University of Nita in YR-28 and went on to get my MBA at Nita State—not too many people from outside of the area know that Nita State is a top twenty-five school for their graduate business program.

After receiving my MBA, I left Nita in YR-24 to work in the Miami design district. By then, I knew I wanted to get in on the business of fashion and import/export. Exciting things were happening in the fashion world at this time, and I was on the cutting edge. My job allowed me to travel the world, work with top designers here in the U.S. and abroad, and use the business skills I learned at Nita State. I made it about ten years in this environment. I loved it but I also knew that it wouldn't last. I was working around the clock and had little time for myself. There was no way I could fit in much of a life outside of work.

In YR-14, I had a really exciting opportunity with NuNu Nectarine, headquartered here in Nita City. NuNu was just starting out but had a strong, almost cult-like following from its small customer base. As you probably know, NuNu specializes in high-end exercise wear. They were looking for innovative fabrics and trying to build their import/export team. I joined their team in exchange for a much-reduced salary. However, because the company was still so small and because it was located in the smaller market of Nita City, the hours were much more conducive to a life outside of work. At this point, I understood that life was more than money, so I made the change, joined the buyer team at NuNu, and came back home to Nita.

I met Ryan, an elementary school teacher, when I moved back to Nita. We were married in YR-13 and had our first child in YR-11. Since that time, we have added two more kids to our family (YR-9 and YR-6).

I initially joined NuNu because of the exciting opportunity that I saw for the growth and success of the company. Plus, I really liked their emphasis on health and lifestyle. I was content with sacrificing salary for lifestyle because they couldn't afford to pay me much in those early days. How things changed! After I joined in YR-14, the company's popularity skyrocketed, expanding well beyond its roots of exercise wear. Our buyer team was amazingly successful and busy—it still wasn't at the level of my days in the Miami design district, but life slowly became more and more hectic with lots of international travel. With Ryan's job grounded here in Nita, we didn't feel that the kids suffered with my traveling and work schedule. Plus, my salary continued to go up and opportunities for even more advancements were right around the corner. At the time of the accident, I was earning $350,000 a year and looking to move up to chief buyer because my long-time boss and mentor, Max O'Brien, had announced his intention to retire at the end of calendar YR-2. Everyone knew I was next in line for the position. His yearly salary was close to seven figures because it included significant stock options.

September 4, YR-2, was a day like many others. I was way too busy at the job and had been at work since before it was light. We were working on a major deadline for a new product line and my team was working around the clock. It was my oldest son's ninth birthday that day, so I was anxious to get home on time to celebrate with him. The NuNu headquarters is right in the middle of the city center. At that time, we lived downtown in a large loft located just six blocks away from the office—I loved walking to work, and that style of commute was right in line with NuNu's philosophy of exercise and sustainability. Ryan had asked me to pick up balloons for Sam's birthday on my way home from work, so I made an unusual stop at a downtown party store, which was a block or two out of my way, to get a dozen yellow balloons, my son's favorite color.

My family was supposed to be sitting down for a birthday dinner at 6:00 p.m. and I, as usual, was running late. It was typical for me to try and cram way too many things into my day. I have often been called a multi-tasker—and I'm a successful one, I might add. I left the party store right at 6:00 (I know because I had been anxious about getting home and was checking my watch). The party store is located on Broadway, a few doors to the north of the corner of Broadway and Washington. I remember walking to the corner and waiting for the walk signal to turn green for my direction. I was juggling the balloons, my laptop bag, and my phone. O'Brien had just sent an emergency text about a snag in our upcoming order processing. I was in the middle of responding to him when the pedestrian crossing signal turned green for walkers. Of course I was using the crosswalk, I am a rule follower through and through. I don't think I was the first person to step out in the street, but I can't be sure. I know there were other people around me because it was right in the middle of the evening commute. I know the light was green for me because I was watching intensely in my hurry to get home. I was texting right before I started walking, not while I was walking. I always look both ways before I cross the street—I have three kids of my own and we drill this into their heads all the time. I would never step out without looking, no matter how hurried or stressed I was. Yes, I would say I was both hurried and stressed in that moment.

As soon as I stepped out in the street, I heard the sound of brakes and I felt my things go flying. The force of the impact to the left-hand side of my body launched me about ten feet, well beyond the crosswalk. I remember being most concerned about the balloons that I saw drifting away as I lay on the ground. The driver of the car got out and came running my way. I was lying on the street and didn't know whether I could get up. I heard the driver say to me, "What have I done? I don't know where you came from! All of a sudden you were there. Oh, what have I done?" I remember thinking I must be pretty badly hurt because the driver seemed really upset. The ambulance and the police seemed to get there quickly, and I was whisked away to General Hospital. I remember asking the paramedics to call Ryan so that the family would know why I was late. The rest of that evening is a blur of x-rays, admissions, and doctors. Looking back at it all, I know that I was in shock. I didn't even see Ryan or the kids until the next day. I completely missed my son's birthday.

Overall, I was pretty lucky with my injuries—I could have been killed. I twisted my left knee, broke my pelvis, and got a hematoma on my left leg. I was told that I wouldn't need surgery but that my injuries would take some rehabilitation to get better and that I may get early arthritis in my knee. I also hit my head in the fall; I suffered a severe concussion and had to get stitches in the back of my head. With any severe concussion and traumatic brain injury (TBI), there is a chance of future brain complications or early onset dementia. My doctors have talked with me about this risk. For the first six months after the accident I experienced intense migraines (I have no migraine history) which made it almost impossible to be around people, stress, or loud noises. Although I feel fine today, the idea of being physically or mentally limited in the future scares me, especially the unknown nature of the timing or severity—how do you plan your life when you don't know whether you'll wake up one morning and not even recognize the people you love?

My rehabilitation process was life-changing for me. I remained in the rehabilitation facility for two weeks. I went home in the middle of September with a walker and immediately started physical therapy. I went to physical therapy twice a week for the first few weeks and then once a week into November. The migraines and my aches and pains made it impossible to work that fall. I continued to see my neurologist, Dr. Campbell, and with his recommendation, I started back to work with reduced hours in November, but never really got back into the full swing of things. The stress, the noise, the schedule, and the human interaction all triggered migraines. It was too much. In January YR-1, O'Brien announced his replacement for chief buyer, and it went to one of my less-experienced colleagues. I understood the decision, but at the time I was disappointed. I know it was a direct result of the accident and my injuries. I officially resigned in February YR-1, but I hadn't been fully engaged since the accident. About that same time, I was feeling much better physically (although still getting the occasional migraine) and began going on long runs to think and be by myself. The solitary nature of running seemed to help with the migraines.

Dr. Campbell prescribed Sumatriptan for the migraines and I have been taking this, plus over-the-counter acetaminophen when they get bad. The medication seems to be controlling the migraines. When I first got out of the hospital, I was having severe migraines every few days. They started getting less frequent a few months after the accident, but I had some remaining brain fog and dizziness. I seemed to be more sensitive to light and loud noises. I was also getting a lot more overwhelmed with work. Since quitting my job in February YR-1, I have probably only had a half-dozen migraines. In addition to the medication, Dr. Campbell said I could control the migraines with cardio exercise, cognitive exercises, and psychological counseling. The cardio is no problem for me. I do cognitive exercises every once in a while, less now than right after the accident. I have not sought any counseling; running is all the therapy I need.

I started my blog, "Recovering Workaholic," the day I quit my job. In the beginning, it was a way for our family to communicate my recovery progress to extended family and close friends but it got passed around to others and the following grew. Today I have close to 200,000 page views a month and I earn a modest salary for that "work." Ryan and I see this as a fluke, a gift, and we know there is no guarantee it will last.

Today my life is at a 180-degree turn from where I was at the time of the accident. My old co-workers don't even recognize me. Before the accident I was a recreational runner and would try to fit a few three- or four-mile runs in each week. The length of my runs grew throughout my recovery, and I plugged into the ultramarathoning community. Initially, I began these longer runs as a way to recover physically and to have some solitude away from the migraine triggers of people and noise. After healing, the running became a way of life for me, and I have participated in three ultramarathons since the accident. My blog continues to gain followers and what started as a recovery diary is now a money-making enterprise. My journey from overworked corporate executive to almost-fifty-year-old ultramarathoner and health guru has hit a chord. It turns out there are many other people out there who are inspired by my story. My writings, sponsorships, and local speaking appearances help pay the bills. Plus, it doesn't feel at all like work. If this continues at its current pace, we expect to pull in close to $100,000 next year, which will be a great supplement to Ryan's teaching job. We have now moved out of downtown and have a great house with more land away from the hustle and bustle of the city. There are days that I miss NuNu and my more high-powered lifestyle. And of course we miss the extra income. But now I have time for my passions: running and spending time with my family.

Despite all of this, every day I am concerned and anxious about my future and my ability to support my family. The business world was my life, and I don't think I will ever have the mental capacity to go back to it. My doctors say the migraines will come back if I return to the long hours and high stress environment. The blog and the ultramarathoning are great for now but I have no illusions that they will last much longer. I am getting older each day and I feel more and more stiffness in my hip related to my injuries. My doctors also tell me that I am likely to develop arthritis in the knee I injured. In short, my current situation is not sustainable. I suspect I have, at most, five years left at this pace.

I contacted Alex Miller, the driver of the car that hit me, a few months after the accident. Miller had sent me flowers while I was in the hospital after the crash, and I thought that was a classy move. During my recovery, I was bored at home and decided to do some internet searching to learn more about the person responsible for my predicament. In November or December YR-2, I found a SupportMe fundraising page for Miller and Miller's spouse. It turns out this accident was tough on Alex Miller too. Miller has a really sad story and was driving for KarPül to make ends meet and help a spouse who was suffering from cancer. The accident really shook Miller up and prevented work with KarPül. I gave $100 on the SupportMe page under my mother's maiden name, T. McGuiness. I felt sorry for their situation, and I know every little bit helps. I did not feel at all responsible for what Miller was going through but I'm human.

I also wrote a note to Alex Miller in February YR-1 to try and heal any guilt Miller might have been feeling—no one deserves that burden. I told Miller that I was sorry for the situation and the accident. I was feeling a new clarity and peace in my life, and I guess I was wanting to share this with others. To be clear, I was apologizing for the situation, not my fault.

I decided to bring this lawsuit because I understood that KarPül may be on the hook for my damages since Miller was driving for KarPül at the time the accident happened. I learned about this possible responsibility from Dr. Campbell. He introduced me to my attorney, B. Anita. It is not my intent to further harm Miller, but I thought if KarPül was picking up the bill, why not? Isn't this what insurance is for?

Deposition Transcript—Alex Miller
October 2, YR-1

My name is Alex Miller. I am thirty years old and live with my spouse, Kai Miller. We have no children. We reside at 6262 Fox Hunt Street in Nita City. I graduated from Boulder High School in YR-13 and then was enlisted in the Army until YR-6. Now, I am a full-time barista at Coffee Cup and I work for Home Base on the side. I used to drive for KarPül, but I don't anymore. My spouse does not work and is currently in remission from thyroid cancer and looking for a job.

Kai and I grew up in Boulder, Colorado. We lived just a few streets away from each other but didn't meet until we were eighteen and graduating from high school. At that time, we were both interested in going into the military for very different reasons. I had always been a disaster at school. I should have been diagnosed with ADD and dyslexia way back in elementary school, but somehow I flew under the radar. It was a wonder I graduated at all. I knew I wasn't cut out for college, so I attended a military recruiting meeting and felt like the Army would be a good fit. I met Kai at that meeting too but Kai, unlike me, was an amazing student without many family resources, so WestPoint was on the horizon. Kai got into WestPoint, and we kept in touch during those four years apart.

At eighteen, I went into basic combat training for ten months. I got my assignment as a Motor Transport Operator and spent seven weeks of advanced training in vehicle operations, loading and unloading, and map reading. I served four years in active duty in areas around the U.S. As a Motor Transport Operator, I was part of the Army's transportation logistics team. I supervised and operated vehicles, transported cargo, and provided advanced mobility for different drills.

When Kai graduated from WestPoint and I finished with my active-duty obligation, we reconnected and married in YR-8. I began my time in the reserves, where I served out my required time and received an honorable discharge. I wasn't cut out for a lifetime of military service, but I am grateful for the opportunities it provided me. Now I've got this long hair and work outside of the military.

Kai was a different story. After graduating from WestPoint, Kai was commissioned as a second lieutenant in the Army and was assigned to the finance branch. The required eight years of service had almost expired when we needed to seek a medical discharge for Kai because of the cancer diagnosis. We are really fortunate to continue to receive good medical benefits through the VA, but Kai has not been able to work since the beginning of YR-2. After we beat this thing, Kai is hoping to get a civilian job in finance here in Nita City.

Now, without Kai's salary, I am working two jobs to support us. Cost of living is high here in Nita City. We've thought about moving, but we really like it here and we've built our own community. Plus, Kai's oncologist is here in Nita, and we are not ready to move away from that yet. I began working at Coffee Cup as soon as we moved here in YR-6. They give me a lot of hours and they offer great benefits. It was a good supplementary source of income when Kai was still actively working. After the diagnosis in January YR-2, I began driving with KarPül in my spare time. I figured this was right up my alley because I had lots of experience and training driving in the military. After driving in those stressful situations, how bad could driving people around town be? The application process to be a driver was intense, definitely more than I had to go through to join the Army! My driving record is clean with no prior accidents before this one and no tickets, so I was able to become a KarPül driver.

KarPül recommended that its drivers increase their insurance coverage, but I always kept mine at the lowest allowed amount. At the time of the incident on September 4, YR-2, I didn't have the additional rideshare insurance. KarPül didn't require it and we simply didn't have the extra money to get it. Plus, I understood that KarPül provided add-on insurance coverage for anything that might happen while I was working if our own insurance wasn't enough. My car is a YR-6 Toyota Camry and I kept it clean and regularly maintained—it was important to me to keep my KarPül riders safe and happy, so I would continue to get good reviews.

The accident happened on September 4, YR-2. In the weeks before that day, my life was going along at a breakneck speed. I had been working my maximum hours at Coffee Cup and I had been getting all of the driving hours that I could with KarPül. In total I was probably averaging sixty or seventy working hours a week between the two jobs and then doing some caretaking for Kai whenever I was home. I know it wasn't healthy and probably wasn't sustainable, but Kai was powering through the last rounds of chemo and I wanted to do my part. Plus, the doctors had been really positive about the progress, and I was secretly saving up for a vacation to Mexico to celebrate the end of our journey—Kai was beating cancer!

The night before the accident, I hadn't gotten a lot of sleep; but I had learned to get by on about six hours a night—I've realized that I don't need a ton of sleep to be productive and get things done. On the morning of September 4, YR-2, I had the opening shift at Coffee Cup, which began at 5:00 a.m. I worked until 2:00 and then immediately began my KarPül driving shift. One perk of working for a coffee shop is that I get to stay pretty caffeinated, for free, throughout the day. I typically drink about six cups of coffee a day and that day was no exception. I may have even had an extra energy drink during my KarPül shift. I usually did. I was about to wrap up my day when I got the ping request to take a rider to the airport. This was always a good trip and usually results in a hefty tip, so I decided to do the one last job. My mistake.

First, I got lost trying to find my rider. Even though I have lived in Nita City for several years now, I still get confused between West Washington Street and Washington Street. Plus, I think the rider may have input the wrong address. Anyway, I finally realized my mistake, called the rider, and convinced him to wait for me. I may have sounded a bit desperate because I was tired and needed the extra money for this ride. I was in a bit of a hurry to get to the rider so he wouldn't drop his request and find someone else. I guess you could say I was hurrying to get there; but I was also following all the rules of the road. I needed this job. I remember driving on Washington and approaching the corner of Broadway and Washington. Washington is a one-way street. I was driving toward the west in the far-right lane because my rider was located on Washington, just past the intersection, in front of the Florence Hotel.

I remember entering the intersection just as the light turned yellow. I could not have safely stopped before entering the intersection. I was probably going about twenty miles per hour, slower than usual, because the setting sun was in my eyes and I was looking for the rider I was picking up. Plus, it was rush hour and there were a lot of people and cars on the street. There is no way that my light had turned red by the time I was crossing the crosswalk. It wouldn't have taken that long. All of a sudden, out of nowhere, I saw the pedestrian right in front of my car. I slammed on my brakes but still made impact. I know because I heard the impact and when I looked, I could no longer see the pedestrian in front of my car. I ran out into the road and didn't care if there were other cars around. I couldn't believe I had hit someone. I was worried about the person I hit and also worried about my job with KarPül. I know this sounds unreasonable, but I really needed that job. I never felt that I did anything wrong. I remember talking with the person I hit and getting a pretty quick response. The pedestrian did not lose consciousness at any time right after the accident. I was relieved that there didn't seem to be anything majorly wrong.

Before I knew it the ambulance was there, and they were taking the pedestrian away to get checked out at the local hospital. I also spoke with the police officer and told them about what happened. I don't know what happened to the rider I was supposed to pick up. I was very shaken up after the accident. In fact, the police officer had me perform a sobriety test on the side of the road which I of course passed. I had not had any alcohol or drugs prior to the accident, I was just shaky from all of the events of the day. When I got home, Kai was so worried about me. I was really upset. Kai suggested that I send some flowers to the hospital for the pedestrian that I hit. I did bring flowers to the hospital with my regards and my hopes for a speedy recovery. No, I never apologized because I had nothing to apologize for. When dropping off the flowers, I asked the nurse about Chen's condition and was told that Chen's worst injury was the fractured pelvis and that the head injury I had been concerned about was very mild and shouldn't cause any major problems. No, I don't remember the nurse's name.

In the weeks following the accident, I was really haunted by the events. I had to file a report about the accident with KarPül and I kept having nightmares where things turned out much worse. I couldn't take my normal shifts at Coffee Cup and I wasn't driving for KarPül. Our friends set up a SupportMe page for donations because they knew we were living paycheck to paycheck. Thanks to the generosity of our friends and family, we were able to get through that time. No, I didn't know that Taylor Chen donated to our SupportMe page.

I was able to return to my normal work schedule at Coffee Cup by the end of YR-2. I don't drive for KarPül anymore. This experience was too traumatizing for that. However, I got a second job at Home Base where I sell tools and other products for home improvement. Kai is now in remission and looking for a job in finance. Although it was delayed, we were finally able to take that trip to Mexico this past summer, which was great for both of us.

Oh yeah, in February YR-1, I got a letter from Taylor Chen. I guess the accident really changed Taylor's life. Although the letter didn't come right out and thank me, it did make clear that the accident put Taylor's life in perspective and opened up doors that have led to positive changes. The letter also really helped with my own feelings of guilt because Taylor recognized that the accident may have been because of the rush and busyness that was a normal part of that corporate lifestyle. I knew the accident was not my fault.

DEPOSITION TRANSCRIPT—KARPÜL RIDER JESSE SMITH DECEMBER 2, YR-1

My name is Jesse Smith. I am sixty years old and live by myself in Chicago, Illinois. I am not married and do not have children. My address is 105 Lake View Drive in Chicago. I am an asset manager at a large, international investment firm. On September 4, YR-2, I was in Nita City for an investment conference. At the time of the incident, I was standing on Washington Street waiting for my KarPül driver to take me to the airport to return to Chicago. I had been in Nita City for three days.

I logged into the KarPül app around 5:45 p.m. to look for a driver to take me to the airport. I was a little delayed in leaving the conference, having run into a few colleagues on my way out the door. My flight was scheduled to leave Nita City at 7:30 p.m. and even though the airport was only twenty miles away, it was rush hour and I was concerned about being late. I got matched with a driver right away and expected the driver to arrive within a few minutes to pick me up. I took a screen shot of my KarPül request because I've gotten burned by this in the past when the driver doesn't show up. About five minutes later I got a call from the driver, Alex Miller, and he asked where I was. I guess I entered the wrong street for pickup, West Washington Street, instead of where I actually was, Washington Street. He told me he was only a few minutes away, so I agreed to wait. He didn't sound stressed or upset when I talked to him; he reassured me he would be right there.

I was waiting on Washington, on the curb outside of the Florence Hotel, about fifteen to twenty yards away from the corner of Broadway and Washington. I was on the north side of the street. I remember the sun setting to my right (west) because it was really bright and difficult to look in that direction. I kept my back towards it and was facing towards the Broadway/Washington intersection. It was about 6:00 by this time and I was feeling impatient and anxious for the driver to get there.

I was watching towards the oncoming traffic, looking for the blue Toyota that was supposed to pick me up when I first noticed the person I now know as Taylor Chen. The first thing I noticed was the bundle of yellow helium balloons that the person was carrying. It made for quite a scene. I think there were around a dozen of them. Then, I noticed that the person carrying the balloons was dressed in business clothes and, even from my distance, appeared stressed. The person kept looking at their phone and seemed to be watching for the lights controlling the Broadway traffic to turn yellow then red so that it would be time to cross. I remember laughing to myself because I could relate to this mindset. I spent a lot of years feeling I was too busy to wait for anything in my forties and fifties. Getting older gives you some perspective, I guess.

There were a lot of people on the sidewalk and lots of cars in the street at that time of day. Nita City is no Chicago but there is still some rush hour traffic. As soon as the light for oncoming traffic turned red, the person I was watching with the balloons stepped off the curb. I'm assuming the walk signal was green for that direction, but I couldn't see it from my angle. I don't know whether they looked to the left before crossing. Other pedestrians stepped off at the same time, but this one was the fastest, true to form and no one else was hit, everyone else managed to see the car in time and get out of the way.

The next things that I saw and heard happened really quickly. I first heard the sound of brakes squealing and then I saw a blue car go through the intersection. It wasn't going too fast, maybe fifteen or twenty miles per hour—due to the traffic it couldn't have gone much faster than that. The car hit the person in the crosswalk and the person went right down in front of the car. The car stopped and the driver got out to check on the pedestrian. I called 911 and ran over from where I was standing too to see if I could help. There were a couple of other people milling about but once they saw we had it under control, no one else stuck around for long.

The driver seemed shaky and nervous, understandably so. Adrenaline will do that to you. I heard the driver say to the injured pedestrian, "What have I done?" The driver may have said something else, but I can't remember—things were a little chaotic. The pedestrian was awake and talking with us but didn't move much. I heard the pedestrian complain about leg and hip pain and I saw some blood on the head but nowhere else. I couldn't tell how serious it was and we didn't want to move anything just in case we would make it worse. The police and ambulance were there right away. They said the pedestrian was stable and would be okay. I gave a quick statement to the police officer.

Only after things had calmed down, maybe twenty or thirty minutes later, did I think about my KarPül ride. I then put two and two together and realized that my driver was probably the one in the accident—it was a blue Toyota Camry. I quickly decided not to bother the driver, who was still talking to the police, and I put in another KarPül request. I got a driver pretty quickly and made it to the airport in time—it turned out my flight was delayed, and we didn't leave until 8:00 p.m.

Deposition Transcript—Former Boss, Max O'Brien December 10, YR-1

My name is Max O'Brien. I am sixty-eight years old and live with my wife in Nita City. We have two grown children who are married now with children of their own. I am the former chief buyer for NuNu Nectarine but I am now enjoying retirement. My address is 6565 Wilmington Lane.

Taylor Chen was also employed at NuNu and we worked together for almost thirteen years in the import/export arm of the company. Taylor joined NuNu in YR-14, back when NuNu was much smaller and less well-known than it is today. I remember Taylor's interview because we had heard about the good work Taylor was doing in Miami and we were looking for an innovative go-getter to join our team. Taylor was just that. Because NuNu is in the exercise wear sector, we are always looking for new, high-performance fabrics being made abroad. Taylor knew this market well and had succeeded in making a name in the high-powered world of the Miami design district. I was impressed and remember thinking that this was just the sort of person we needed.

Taylor took a chance, joining NuNu back in YR-14, and it paid off. Since then, the company has grown and thrived, in part due to the good work of Taylor and our entire buying team. Taylor traveled a lot in this position. I remember giving my own advice about life going fast and enjoying time with the kids while they are still young, but Taylor was headstrong and bent on success. Taylor was a whirlwind of energy, rushing around with many balls in the air. As the company continued to grow, so did Taylor's hours and salary.

On the day of Taylor's accident, we were in the middle of a rush project, which we often are. We were finalizing the new winter line and we had been running into hiccup after hiccup with the shipments. Taylor was responsible for the majority of the overseas shipments, so a lot of this stress was landing squarely on our department and, specifically, on Taylor. I remember getting a call about another shipment delay that would have pushed us past our deadline. I ran down to Taylor's office to find it empty. I was surprised Taylor had left already because we usually work until at least 8:00 in the weeks prior to a product line launch.

I remember texting Taylor with an update on the shipping issue and just got a partial response. I was frustrated and remember calling Ryan Chen (Taylor's spouse) to find out where Taylor was. That was when I learned that Taylor had been involved in a car accident. I understand that Taylor may have been in the middle of texting me when the accident occurred. I feel horrible about the stress I may have caused.

I have walked the streets of Nita City with Taylor Chen many times during our lunch breaks or after work. I have never known Taylor to be reckless as a pedestrian and I can't remember a time when Taylor was texting or using the phone while walking.

I visited Taylor in the hospital after the accident—Taylor always has a positive attitude, but I could tell that the injuries and headaches were causing a lot of pain. I'm glad that the physical recovery is now over.

It's no secret that before the accident, Taylor was next in line for my position of chief buyer for NuNu Nectarine. Taylor had the most seniority in our department and would have been a natural fit for the position. I talked to Taylor about taking over the position for me after my retirement. I had always planned on retiring in January YR-1. After the accident, Taylor came back to work in November YR-2 and I had high hopes for the re-entry. However, it quickly became apparent that Taylor's heart was no longer in it. Taylor said the migraines made it difficult to concentrate but I could also tell that the joy for the work was gone. I ended up recommending another one of our colleagues for chief buyer and Taylor left the company soon after. I can confidently say that were it not for the accident, Taylor Chen would be chief buyer for NuNu Nectarine.

Taylor and I have kept in touch since my retirement. Like everything in Taylor's life, recovery has been a whirlwind. Taylor can do nothing halfway. After feeling better physically, Taylor kept pushing and pushing the limits. Now, instead of working sixty to seventy hours a week, Taylor has embraced a totally new lifestyle as a stay-at-home parent, ultra-marathon runner, and blogger. Taylor seems full of life and happier than I have ever seen.

Medical Records and Reports

GENERAL HOSPITAL
Medical Records

I hereby certify that the attached 3 pages are true and accurate copies of the General Hospital medical records of patient Taylor Chen

Assistant Medical Records Librarian

GENERAL HOSPITAL
Emergency Department

PRESENTING COMPLAINT	Pedestrian / Automobile Accident				Taylor Chen 1015 Silver Stream Rd Nita City, Nita 57819
ARRIVED BY	Ambulance	TIME	18:20		
CONDITION ON ADMISSION	FAIR: X	GOOD:	COMA:	HEMORRHAGE:	
ACCIDENTAL INJURY:	NO:	YES: X	DATE: 09/04/YR-2		
ALLERGIES	NO:	YES:	SPECIFY:		

TIME:	TEMP.	PULSE	RESP.	B.P.	TIME:	TEMP.	PULSE	RESP.	B.P.
18:25	98.8	70	18	120/80	19:10	98.7	66	17	115/78

NURSE'S NOTES: Pt. reports pain in head and hip
Moderate headache. Oriented x3

MEDICATIONS: N/A

NURSE'S SIGNATURE: K. Lansing

HISTORY AND PHYSICAL: **HY:** 47-y-o pedestrian hit by KarPül Driver in Toyota Camry when Camry entered intersection. Pt. did not see car before impact. Complains of headache, pain L. extremities.
EXAM: Multiple minor contusions and abrasions, chest sounds normal, abdomen non-tender, neuro exam shows mild concussion.

DOCTOR'S ORDERS

	CBC		UA
	EKG		CHEST X-RAY
X	Skull x-ray		
X	L pelvis and leg x-ray		
X	Head CT		
	Fractured Pelvis, Other X-rays,		
	CT normal		
	IMMUNIZATION		
	SUTURE NO.		

TREATMENT: Abrasions cleaned and dressed. Stitches in head wound. Watching for signs of post-concussion syndrome. Pelvis stabilized. Admitted to hospital for treatment and observation. Acetaminophen p.r.n.

DIAGNOSIS: Mild closed head injury
Multiple abrasions and contusions, including head wound. Stable pelvis fracture at the Iliac Wing.

DIAGNOSIS CODE:

PHYSICIAN: R Daily, MD

DISCHARGED–CONDITION	TIME:	ADMITTED—ROOM NO. 235	TIME: 22:45

PATIENT'S PHYSICIAN	C. Barron, MD	☐ CONTACTED ____AM/PM	AT ☐ UNABLE TO CONTACT	NOTIFIED: RELATIVE / MEDICAL EXAMINER
REFERRED TO		☐ CONTACTED ____AM/PM	AT ☐ UNABLE TO CONTACT	POLICE / BY: / TIME:
INSTRUCTIONS TO:				DATE:

(PATIENT'S NAME) (HOSPITAL #)

I understand I received emergency care only. I am to call the physician listed below for follow-up care.

Dr. Campbell (Call for appointment)

I also acknowledge that I have received and understand the emergency physician's instructions.

Instructor's Signature ____________________ Patient's signature Taylor Chen

GENERAL HOSPITAL
DISCHARGE SUMMARY

PATIENT: Taylor Chen

ADMISSION DATE: 9/4/YR-2

DISCHARGE DATE: 9/18/YR-2

ATTENDING PHYSICIAN: R. Daily, MD

DISCHARGE DIAGNOSIS: 1. Concussion

2. Head Contusion

3. Fractured Pelvis

4. Strained Knee

DOCTOR'S SUMMARY:

This forty-seven-year-old patient was admitted from the emergency room, where the patient arrived by ambulance from the scene of a pedestrian/automobile incident. Patient was the pedestrian. Patient reported no unconsciousness at the scene. Patient suffered fractured pelvis, strained knee, head contusion requiring stitches (performed in emergency room), and mild to moderate concussion.

History was non-contributory.

On admission, patient was somewhat slow in verbal response, but this resolved within an hour. Vital signs were normal. Physical examination confirmed fractured pelvis on left side of body, strained left knee, head contusion, and mild to moderate concussion. Other than current injuries, patient appears to be healthy, middle-aged person in good physical shape. Patient responded appropriately to commands, but displayed a somewhat flat affect. Not uncommon following an injury event like this one. Examination of the cranial nerves showed pupils that were equally reactive to light and accommodation. The fundus showed no papilledema. Extraocular movements showed no nystagmus. Face was symmetrical on voluntary motion. Motor examination revealed good strength throughout (other than left leg and hip). Coordination testing was normal. CT scan showed mild to moderate concussion.

In consultation with orthopedics, we confirmed that patient's iliac wing pelvic fracture was stable, was not displaced, and did not need repositioning or surgical treatment. Alignment is normal. No other ligament damage. Patient underwent three times daily physical therapy during four days in our care and additional ten days in rehabilitation. Upon discharge, patient can walk assisted by walking aid. Will send patient home with walker and twice weekly physical therapy referral for next ten weeks. Pain medication as needed, although pain appears to be resolving. Knee strain should be treated with rest and physical therapy, also resolving. Should resume normal exercise and movement in next eight to ten weeks. Possibility of future pain in knee in normal aging process, early onset arthritis is possible with injury of this type.

In consultation with neurology, patient was given acetaminophen for pain associated with concussion. We closely observed patient in the first few days following concussion. Patient experienced severe headaches in the days following admission. Headaches have been lessening in severity and duration. Recommend following up with neurologist for continuing treatment.

R Daily, MD

R. Daily, M.D., Attending Physician

EVAN CAMPBELL, M.D.
Nita Neurological Institute, General Hospital
210 5th Avenue, Suite 302
Nita City, Nita
March 12, YR-0

B. Anita
Anita & Associates, LLP
6490 Cascade Street, Suite 105
Nita City, Nita 12345

Re: Taylor Chen

Dear B. Anita:

I have been closely involved in treating your client and my patient since the September 4, YR-2, accident when patient Taylor Chen, a pedestrian, was struck in a crosswalk by a KarPül driver.

Chen was transported by ambulance to General Hospital's emergency department on the evening of September 4, YR-2, and admitted that day. I have reviewed and analyzed all medical reports for this patient related to this incident, including all emergency records, CT scans, notes, test results, discharge reports, rehabilitation records, and medical diagnosis.

I first examined Chen as part of a neurological consultation on September 6, YR-2, while Chen was in General Hospital. In my neurological exam of Chen, I checked mental status, speech, balance, reflexes, and vision. I confirmed the existence of a moderate concussion and mild traumatic brain injury (mTBI) caused by the motor vehicle accident. I performed tests to confirm proper neurological functioning. Chen experienced severe headaches in the days following the event, so I ordered acetaminophen for pain and continued observation. Headaches following a moderate concussion are normal. We look for severe headaches to lessen in duration and nature in the days and weeks following a concussive event. This is often treated by rest and removal of stimuli such as electronics, stressful situations, and loud noises.

I continued to monitor Chen's treatment until discharge from General Hospital's rehabilitation facility on September 18, YR-2. At this time, the headaches were slowly resolving—becoming less frequent and less intense. Post-concussion neurocognitive test scores were also almost back to baseline. Upon discharge, patient was capable of completing activities of daily living. However, Chen was still experiencing post-concussive symptoms and was recommended for follow-up with neurology following discharge. Chen visited my office for this neurological follow-up. I have now seen Chen on five separate occasions since the discharge from General Hospital, the most recent visit being two weeks ago.

There is no precise timeline for concussion recovery. While the majority of patients who experience a moderate concussion/mild traumatic brain injury can be symptom-free within a few weeks after experiencing the injury, for many people concussive symptoms continue. This has been Chen's experience. Since discharge from General Hospital, Chen has continued reporting migraine headaches, difficulty concentrating/brain fog, dizziness, light sensitivity, some memory deficiencies, and feelings of being overwhelmed in a crowded room or in otherwise stressful situations. These symptoms were first treated by continued rest and isolation—the symptoms became less frequent but still present in the months following the incident. I prescribed the migraine medication, Sumatriptan, in addition to acetaminophen as needed.

The brain responds to a mild head injury with inflammation and bruising around the injured area. Swelling and bruising in the brain causes a temporary breakdown of the neurons in the injured area and can disrupt neurovascular coupling, the system of communication between neurons and blood vessels. Post-concussion, the brain's normal communication system can be blocked by inflammation and the brain may use other pathways for this critical communication. Concussion symptoms are a result of this dysfunction of the neurovascular coupling system. After a mild traumatic brain injury, the brain often returns to its normal functioning within several weeks. For some people, the brain continues to use the inefficient processes that it developed, though they should have been temporary. In this case, symptoms can result indefinitely—this is called post-concussion syndrome and presents with many of the symptoms complained of by Chen, including dizziness, headaches, social difficulties, sensitivity to loud noises, and difficulty with memory. Post-concussion syndrome can be treated with cognitive exercises, physical exercise, psychotherapy, and medication, but it may never resolve entirely.

Chen had a high stress career in the fashion industry with NuNu Nectarine prior to the accident. In the weeks after the accident, I strongly recommended that Chen temporarily refrain from returning to work in the hopes of maximizing rest and full recovery. In November YR-2, after confirming that most of the symptoms were resolving, I agreed that Chen could return to work on a reduced-hours basis. Between November YR-2 and February YR-1, Chen reported continued post-concussive symptoms, primarily migraines and sensitivity to crowds and stress. We continued treating these symptoms with medication when needed. Because Chen's orthopedic injuries had resolved, I also recommended at least thirty minutes of cardiovascular exercise daily, cognitive exercises, and psychological counseling to treat Chen's fears associated with her future prognosis: the prolonged post-concussive syndrome, possible early onset of dementia associated with PCS, and also the possibility of early onset arthritis associated with the injuries to Chen's hip and knee. Chen had been a recreational runner prior to the accident, so I recommended running as part of the treatment. Chen has since greatly exceeded the recommended minimum of daily exercise and is involved in ultramarathons. I believe that this exercise is one of the reasons that the post-concussive symptoms have been so well-controlled. I'm not sure whether Chen has engaged in the cognitive exercises. I asked Chen about the recommended psychological counseling and understand that there has been no follow-up in this area.

Chen suffers from post-concussion syndrome and may continue to suffer from this disease for the remainder of the life span. Suffering a concussion can also increase risk of developing Parkinson's Disease by 50 percent, permanent memory damage, and dementia. For some patients, a return to pre-concussion life is not possible. Post-concussion syndrome can limit a patient's ability to work and socialize. I currently examine Chen on a yearly basis to monitor symptoms and medication. I will continue to do so. Very little can be done to treat post-concussive syndrome other than managing symptoms with lifestyle and medication. Chen seems to be doing both of these things successfully at the moment. I understand from our recent visit that Chen has not experienced any migraines or post-concussive symptoms in the past six months. However, I think that this is due to the increased physical activity and the removal of stress. I have no doubt that Chen could be at higher risk of these post-concussive symptoms reappearing were Chen to return to work at NuNu Nectarine.

EVAN CAMPBELL, M.D.
Nita Neurological Institute, General Hospital
210 5th Avenue, Suite 302
Nita City, Nita

EDUCATION & TRAINING:

B.A., University of California, Berkeley, YR-25

M.A., University of Nita, YR-23

M.D., University of Nita, YR-20

PRESENT POSITIONS

- Chief, Neurosurgery Service, Chairman, Department of Neurology
- Director, Service of Sports Medicine and Concussion
- Clinical Professor Neurology and Neurosurgery, University of Nita
- Co-Founder and Co-Director, Nita Neurological Institute
- Consultant to NFL Concussion Committee

FELLOWSHIPS:

YR-10 **Fellow,** American College of Sports Medicine

YR-8 **Fellow,** American Association Neurological Surgeons (FAANS)

PROFESIONAL MEMBERSHIPS AND AWARDS:

- American College of Sports Medicine, Nita Chapter (YR-18 to present)
- Editorial Board, Exercise and Sports Science Reviews (YR-5 to present)
- Assoc. of Neurological Surgeons, Chair, Sports Medicine Section (YR-7 to present; Chair, YR-2 to present)
- American Academy of Sports Physicians
- Nita Scholastic Federation Award, YR-11
- United States Sports Academy, Sports Medicine Award (YR-4)

REPRESENTATIVE PUBLICATIONS:

- History of Concussions, ACSM Annual Meeting
- Diagnosis and Management of Concussion, Sports Medicine Essentials
- Return to Play Guidelines After Concussion, Neuro-Athlete Foundation

SPECIALTY BOARD CERTIFICATION:

American Board of Neurological Surgery, YR-20

Quinn Cameron, M.D.
River Front Professional Building
677 Walnut Street
Nita City, Nita

April 6, YR-0

Re: Taylor Chen

C. Harris
HARRIS, MATHERS & ROSS, LLP
1600 Janan Place, Suite 200
Nita City, Nita 12345
Email: charris@HMR.com
Dear C. Harris:

Pursuant to your request of March 18, YR-0, I have reviewed the material you forwarded to me, including the General Hospital Emergency Department records, CT Scans, Test Results, Discharge Summary, and the report of Dr. Campbell, dated March 12, YR-0. I have also reviewed photographs of the car post-incident, the depositions of Taylor Chen and Max O'Brien, and the police accident report.

There are a number of sound medical reasons that lead me to believe that, although Taylor Chen may have experienced a mild or even moderate concussion, Chen can be expected to resume a normal life and there is great evidence to support that Chen is already doing so. There is no medical relationship between the incident of September 4, YR-2, and the current symptoms that Chen is reporting.

A concussion can be caused by a blow, bump, fall, or hit that jars the brain within the skull. Often a moderate to severe concussion also involves a loss of consciousness. It is important to note here that Chen did not report any loss of consciousness the day of the incident. Nor is any loss of consciousness included in the medical records or reports. This indicates that Chen most likely experienced a mild concussive event.

Approximately 80 percent of concussions resolve over seven to fourteen days, with the average being ten days. People with concussions should not return to normal physical activity or electronic screens for one week after sustaining the injury. There are two phases to recovery from a concussion: the acute phase and the recovery phase. During the acute phase of concussion recovery (lasting approximately one week), the brain needs mental and physical rest in order to fully and effectively recover. Absence from school or work is recommended in order to give the brain a break from focus, memory, and concentration—all of these neurological processes can be temporarily affected by a concussion. Rest is recommended to help expedite the time of the healing process.

Here, Chen was in the hospital and associated rehabilitation facility for physical injuries for fourteen days, primarily for the fractured pelvis. There is considerable evidence that would indicate that the incident injury of September 4, YR-2, was actually a relatively minor one with regards to the brain and would not be productive of the risk factors associated with any long-term complications associated with a severe concussion or repeated moderate concussions. However, if any brain trauma was related to the incident in question, it would be a mild to moderate concussion, and any associated symptoms would resolve in seven to ten days. As expected, the records show that Chen's concussion symptoms were resolving in the two weeks following the incident. For any symptoms occurring during this acute phase, over-the-counter pain medication, ice applied to head and neck, and sleep or rest would be recommended. All of these things were prescribed and done by Chen in this initial acute phase.

During the second, recovery phase, the patient will feel physical improvement, such as headaches or dizziness subsiding and post-concussion neurocognitive test scores will show improvement. Mild concussions result in short-term symptoms that go away with time. Chen's reported recovery process was almost textbook in this regard. Concussion symptoms were resolving, and neurocognitive test scores were almost back to normal at the time of discharge. During this phase, patients can gradually return to work and physical activity. There may still be some residual headaches linked to loud noises, mental processing, and memory. This will resolve.

A very small percentage of patients enter into a chronic phase where patients may experience longer-lasting problems with cognitive function. Severe or repetitive concussions are the ones more likely to result in long-term consequences. This is not the case here. I don't believe that Chen has entered into this chronic phase, nor would entry into the chronic phase be expected with this mild brain injury. Once recovered, it is not possible for a patient to regress without additional neurological trauma. Chen's neurocognitive test scores were good on September 18, YR-2, and the reported symptoms had all but resolved. There is no reason to suspect that this injury incident had anything to do with any currently reported symptoms, in fact the science supports the opposite conclusion.

Dr. Campbell opines that Chen suffers from chronic post-concussion syndrome. I do not agree with this assessment. This is a very rare diagnosis and has received considerable attention due to NFL players diagnosed with this condition after repeated, severe concussions. It is no coincidence that Dr. Campbell is a consultant to the NFL. According to published research, it takes an average of seventeen concussions to lead to chronic post-concussion syndrome. Risk factors associated with chronic post-concussion syndrome are loss of consciousness at the time of injury, clinical evidence of brain injury beyond mTBI, neurocognitive test scores well below those reported for Chen, skull fracture, and/or repeated moderate concussions. The evidence here shows none of these elevated risk factors. Indeed, the fact that the symptoms were resolving and post-concussion neurocognitive test scores were almost back to normal is evidence against any causal relationship.

A mild to moderate concussion, like the one Taylor Chen experienced, is a mild traumatic brain injury. Concussion symptoms, such as the headaches initially experienced by Chen, will dissipate with time and are treatable. Chen's ability to engage in work following the injury incident, even on a reduced hours basis, the long-distance running, engagement in family life, writing, and blogging, are all evidence that Chen is not experiencing a chronic neurological condition. To the extent Chen experienced any concussive symptoms, they had resolved by the time of discharge from General Hospital, September 18, YR-2.

Thank you for referring this file to me. Further record review and consultation time will be billed at our customary rate of $850 an hour. Deposition time will be billed at $900 an hour with a four-hour minimum. Trial time will be billed at $6,000 per trial day or any portion thereof. Enclosed per your request is a copy of my curriculum vitae.

Sincerely,

Q. Cameron, M.D.

Quinn Cameron, M.D.
River Front Professional Building
677 Walnut Street
Nita City, Nita

EDUCATION AND TRAINING:

- University of San Diego, BS YR-18
- Yale University, MD YR-14
- Scripps Clinic, San Diego, California, Residency in Neurology, YR-13–YR-10

ARMED SERVICE:

- Balboa Naval Hospital, San Diego, California, Staff Neurologist, YR-10–YR-7

PRACTICE:

- Nita City: Private Practice in Neurology, YR-7 to date

LICENSURE:

- California, Nita

PROFESSIONAL AFFILIATIONS:

- American Medical Association
- Nita Medical Society
- American Board of Neurology & Psychiatry—Certified in Neurology
- Nita Neurological Society, President YR-3–YR-1
- International Society of Neurology

MEDICAL EDUCATION ACTIVITIES:

- University of Nita Medical School, Clinical Instructor in Neurology, YR-7 to date

PUBLICATIONS:

- Author or co-author of eighteen articles on neurology

EXHIBITS

Exhibit 1

Newspaper Article

KarPül Krash Kauses Katastrophe

September 10, YR-2

Taylor Chen, textile buyer for high-end fashion brand Nu Nu Nectarine, was struck by a vehicle while in a crosswalk last week in Nita City. Chen was walking from the Nu Nu Nectarine headquarters to the Chen family's downtown loft after a long day at the office. It was Chen's oldest son's birthday that day and Chen had stopped off to buy a bunch of yellow balloons to bring home for the family dinner celebration.

Eyewitnesses say that Chen was crossing the street when hit in the crosswalk by a KarPül driver. Witnesses dispute whether the light was green for the driver or the pedestrian. Chen suffered injuries to the hip and head and remains in the hospital today.

Although there was no KarPül rider in the car at the time of the accident, records show that the KarPül driver had engaged with a potential rider and was on the way to pick up that rider when the crash occurred. The accident, increasingly common in its circumstances, points to the growing controversy between rideshare drivers and those that share the roadway with them in Nita City.

When it comes to ridesharing companies, the issue of liability has yet to be settled by the courts. Rideshare drivers may have different levels of responsibility based on what they are doing at the time of the accident. This liability also differs from state to state. Here in Nita, rideshare drivers, like the one involved in this incident, are considered independent contractors and not employees of the rideshare company. This is a significant distinction; when drivers are considered "employees," the employer is directly liable for the employee's negligence under the legal doctrine of *respondeat superior*. But since rideshare drivers are not employees in Nita, rideshare companies are not directly liable for the acts of its drivers. In order to be held liable, the rideshare company would need to be independently liable for its own negligent act, such as improperly hiring an unsafe driver. In Chen's accident, that does not appear to be the case.

This doctrine, however, does not let rideshare companies off the hook. As soon as a request for a ride is accepted and during the entire trip, Nita law requires rideshare companies like KarPül to provide third-party liability coverage up to $1 million for damage to any third party including a passenger, another driver, or a pedestrian, like Chen, injured by the contracted ride-share drivers.

The driver, if found to be at fault, is still liable for damages that the driver caused. However, the driver may be protected by this additional insurance coverage through the rideshare company.

Exhibit 2

Excerpts of Recovering Workaholic Blog by Chen

Recovering Workaholic

February 3, YR-1

Today I quit my job! Tada! Just like that . . .. However, not just like that. This day has been coming for the last several months. I have been on the journey of my lifetime since September 4, YR-2. In fact, to be frank, my job was kind to keep me around as long as they did.

In September of last year I was involved in a car accident. To be clear, I was walking, in a crosswalk, and a car took me out. I guess I was lucky not to have more injuries, but as often as people tell me that, I also think, was this really lucky?

On September 4 of YR-2, the day of the BIG CHANGE, I fractured my pelvis, injured my knee, cracked open my head, had a severe concussion. Life as I knew it was over. I stayed in the hospital for several weeks and for a while there it was touch and go. I knew then that my life would never be the same. When I was finally able to leave the hospital, I had months of intense rehabilitation work to do. Even now, my doctors tell me that I may never be "normal"—whatever that is.

As difficult as that time was, as soon as the accident happened, I experienced a new kind of peace. I was no longer chasing and striving, I couldn't! Since I was a child, I had been striving and swimming upstream—for the best grades, for the best track records, for the best job, the best promotion, the best lifestyle . . . . And I was winning. I was voted most likely to succeed in my graduating class and, in the eyes of the world, I was succeeding! I had a successful job for one of the best companies in America, I was married to a great spouse and I had three beautiful children. However, I never had enough time to do what made life worth living—I had no time with my kids, my spouse and clearly no time for myself.

And now, here I am. Left with more time than I could ever imagine. I would never have chosen this path for myself but here goes nothing. Will I make it? Will the finances work? More importantly, will I even like it? I'm still not sure. Join me in this journey if you are curious. I am.

Exhibit 2a

Recovering Workaholic

February 16, YR-1

Life sure looks different. This morning I put on my running shoes and headed out on the trails before anyone was up. Back when I was working so much, I rarely had time to get out and do anything for myself. Now, I enjoy these moments alone. I feel like I can finally breath. I have decided to keep the kids home from school for the day—a hooky day! We are going to check out the Magic Kingdom—I haven't been there for years, and my kids have never been. Wish me luck!

Exhibit 2b

Recovering Workaholic

March 4, YR-1

Today I signed up for a marathon, I feel incredible! There is no way I could have done this before the BIG CHANGE. But now, why not? I have the time, I am healthier than I have ever been, and I have the support of my family and friends. I'm going to do this thing.

Exhibit 2c

Recovering Workaholic

May 28, YR-1

I am considering filing a lawsuit against KarPül, so this may be my last chance to talk about the BIG CHANGE. Don't worry, I will continue to blog about my runs, my family, my life. My neurologist introduced me to a lawyer that told me that because the driver that hit me was on the clock for KarPül, they may kick in funds if the driver is found responsible. As happy as I am today, there is no question that the BIG CHANGE resulted in a huge loss of money for me and my family. I wouldn't be considering the suit if it were just against the poor guy who hit me. I know that this accident was a big change for him too. He messed up, but didn't mean to do anything bad. Just living his life . . . .

Exhibit 3

Police Report

NITA CITY POLICE DEPARTMENT ACCIDENT REPORT

ACCIDENT LOCATION

COUNTY	CITY	ACCIDENT DATE	TIME
Nita City	Nita	9/4/YR-2	18:00

STREET NAME	FT N S E <u>W</u>	INTERSECTION
Washington Street		Broadway Street

ACCIDENT CONDITIONS

WEATHER	LIGHT	ROAD SURFACE	TOTAL LANES		
(1) CLEAR/CLOUDY 3 RAIN 2 FOG 4 SNOW	(1) DAY 3 ST LTS 2 DAWN/DUSK 4 DARK	(1) DRY 3 SNOW OR ICE 2 WET 4 OTHER	3	1 DIVIDED 2 LIMITED ACCESS 3 OTHER	Y N CONSTRUCTION ZONE; (Y) N INVESTIGATED AT SCENE

VEHICLE DRIVER NO 1

STATE	DRIVER'S LICENSE	DOB	HAZARDOUS ACTION/CITATION	HELMET
Nita	M-878021662323	7/15/YR-31	Y (N)	Y (N)

DRIVER'S NAME First	MI	Last	ADDRESS City	State	AGE	SEX	INJ.
Alex	N.	Miller	6262 Fox Hunt Street	Nita City	29	M	N

YEAR	MAKE	MODEL	TRAILER	REGISTRATION	YR/STATE	VIN	REMOVED TO/BY
YR-6	Toyota	Camry	N	Y	Y-5/NA	PKU 444	Drove Away

Y N HAZ. CITATION	Y N DRIVER RE-EXAM	Y N VEHICLE DEFECT	Y N FUEL LEAKAGE	IMPACT SEVERITY
Y N OTHER CITATION	Y N VISION OBSCTRUCT.	Y N VEHICLE DRIVEABLE	Y N VEHICLE FIRE	

RESTRAINTS BY OCCUPANT'S POS.	NAME	ADDRESS	POS	AGE	SEX	INJ	HELMET
	Alex Miller	above					Y N
1 2 3							Y N
4 5 6							Y N

TOTAL OCCUPANTS	LOCAL OWNER/USER PHONE	INSURANCE CO	AGENCY PHONE	INJURED TAKEN TO/BY
1	888-543-2222	Low Cost Co.		N/A

~~VEHICLE DRIVER NO 2~~ Pedestrian

STATE	DRIVER'S LICENSE	DOB	HAZARDOUS ACTION/CITATION	HELMET
Nita		11/6/YR-50	Y (N)	Y (N)

DRIVER'S NAME First	MI	Last	ADDRESS City	State	AGE	SEX	INJ.
Taylor	N.	Chen	1014 Silver Stream	Nita City	47		Y

YEAR	MAKE	MODEL	TRAILER	REGISTRATION	YR/STATE	VIN	REMOVED TO/BY

Y N HAZ. CITATION	Y N DRIVER RE-EXAM	Y N VEHICLE DEFECT	Y N FUEL LEAKAGE	IMPACT SEVERITY
Y N OTHER CITATION	Y N VISION OBSCTRUCT.	Y N VEHICLE DRIVEABLE	Y N VEHICLE FIRE	

RESTRAINTS BY OCCUPANT'S POS.	NAME	ADDRESS	POS	AGE	SEX	INJ	HELMET
							Y N
1 2 3							Y N
4 5 6							Y N

TOTAL OCCUPANTS	LOCAL OWNER/USER PHONE	INSURANCE CO	AGENCY PHONE	INJURED TAKEN TO/BY

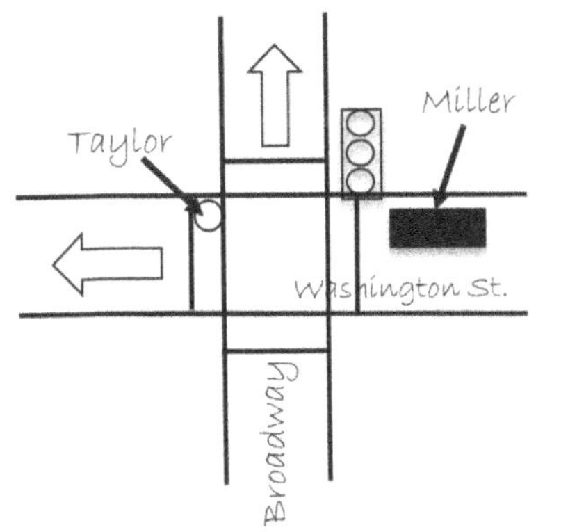

ACCIDENT DESCRIPTION AND REMARKS (EXPLAIN)

Arrived at scene at approximately 18:00 on 9/4/YR-2.
Pedestrian lying in roadway, thrown about 5 feet,
responsive, no loss of consciousness. Driver upset and
shaky.
Performed sobriety test to rule out DUI. No further testing.
Pedestrian taken to General Hospital for abrasions and
minor injuries. Interviewed eyewitness, driver and
pedestrian (summarized in attachments).
No citation

REPORTED: DATE	TIME	INVESTIGATORS	CASE NUMBER
9/4/YR-2	20:30	Brown	NA-456123

DAMAGE TO PROPERTY OTHER THAN VEHICLES

No

NITA CITY POLICE DEPARTMENT
ACCIDENT REPORT
Attachment 1 of 3

INTERVIEW WITH ALEX MILLER

Miller is 29 years old and was driving with KarPül rideshare at the time of the accident. Miller was the driver that hit the pedestrian in the crosswalk. Miller is insistent about not seeing pedestrian prior to incident. Miller reports having the green light prior to the intersection and saw the light turn yellow on passing through the intersection. Miller seems sure that pedestrian crossed while light was yellow in direction of driving. Miller reports setting sun may have been factor.

Miller states that prior to the accident, had been working for 15 hours. Witness reports having no alcohol or drugs prior to incident, but only coffee and energy drink. I performed a roadside sobriety test based on the appearance of witness: shaky, pale, upset. Witness passed sobriety test and determined no further testing is needed. Witness is clearly upset due to the incident and reports a need to get home to sick spouse. Witness agrees to come to station next day to give fuller interview.

*Witness appeared at station on September 5, YR-2. Further interview is consistent with initial interview. No need for follow-up. Witness requested location of hospital for Chen. Cooperative.

NITA CITY POLICE DEPARTMENT
ACCIDENT REPORT
Attachment 2 of 3

INTERVIEW WITH JESSE SMITH

Smith is 59 years old. Witness approached officer while interviewing Miller. Witness reported seeing pedestrian with yellow balloons prior to incident. Pedestrian had appeared hurried and anxious to cross the street. Pedestrian was on phone. Pedestrian darted out into street immediately when walk signal turned green. Other pedestrians followed victim. Requested that witness sign a statement, but declined to do so because late for flight.

NITA CITY POLICE DEPARTMENT
ACCIDENT REPORT
Attachment 3 of 3

INTERVIEW WITH TAYLOR CHEN

Interviewed witness at General Hospital. Witness gave signed statement (attached).

WITNESS STATEMENT

I, Taylor Chen, am ~~49~~ 47 TC years old and live in Nita City. I am a full-time employee at NuNu Nectarine where I work in import/export.

I was working on September 4, YR-2, and was walking home from work at approximately 6:00 p.m. when I was hit by a car in a crosswalk. I was watching for traffic and remember the walk signal turning green for my direction. Other pedestrians were crossing the street at the same time I crossed. I was in a hurry to get home to my family to celebrate my son's ninth birthday. I did not see the car before it struck me. I immediately remember feeling pain in my hip and my head.

I have read the above paragraphs, and they are an accurate transcription of what I have said to Officer Brown. To the best of my knowledge, the statement is true and accurate.

Signed: *Taylor Chen*

Witness: Officer Brown

Exhibit 4

Letter from Chen to Miller

February 14, YR-1

Dear Alex,

My name is Taylor Chen and I am the person that you hit in the crosswalk back in September. I wanted to send you a note in case you ever thought about me or wondered how I was doing. The recovery process has been difficult but, in short, I'm doing great. In some ways, the accident opened up doors I didn't even know needed opening. Maybe I should thank you? ☺

Anyway, I understand that the process hasn't been easy for you or your family either. I'm sorry for that and for my part in it. I'm happy to say that my life is much less hurried now and I am altogether less distracted. Life is good.

I wish you all the best,

Taylor

Exhibit 5

Diagram of Accident Scene

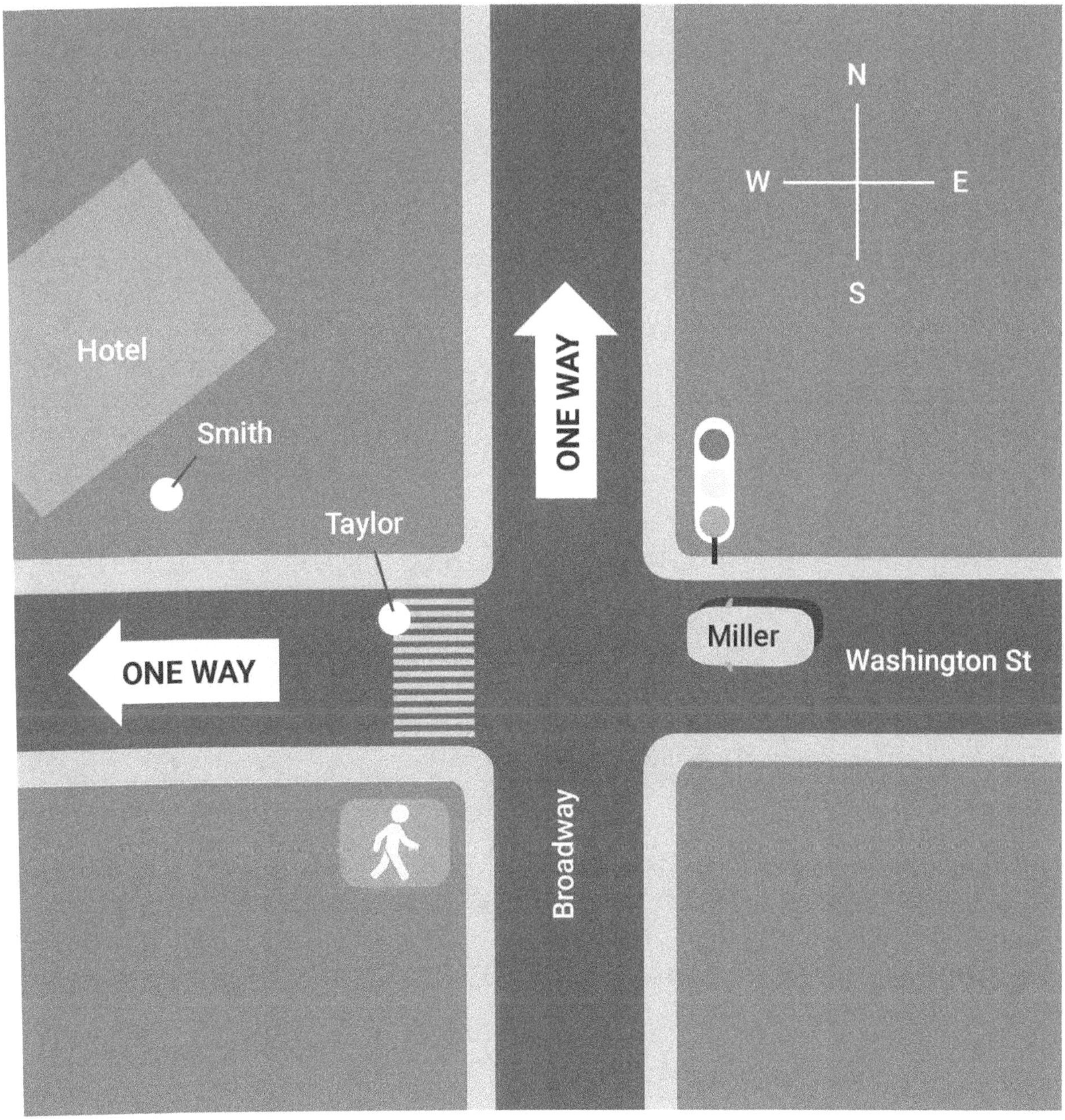

Exhibit 6

Screen Shot of Texts Between Chen and O'Brien

Exhibit 7

FLORIST NOTE FROM MILLER TO CHEN

Exhibit 8

KarPül Screen Shot—Pick-up Request

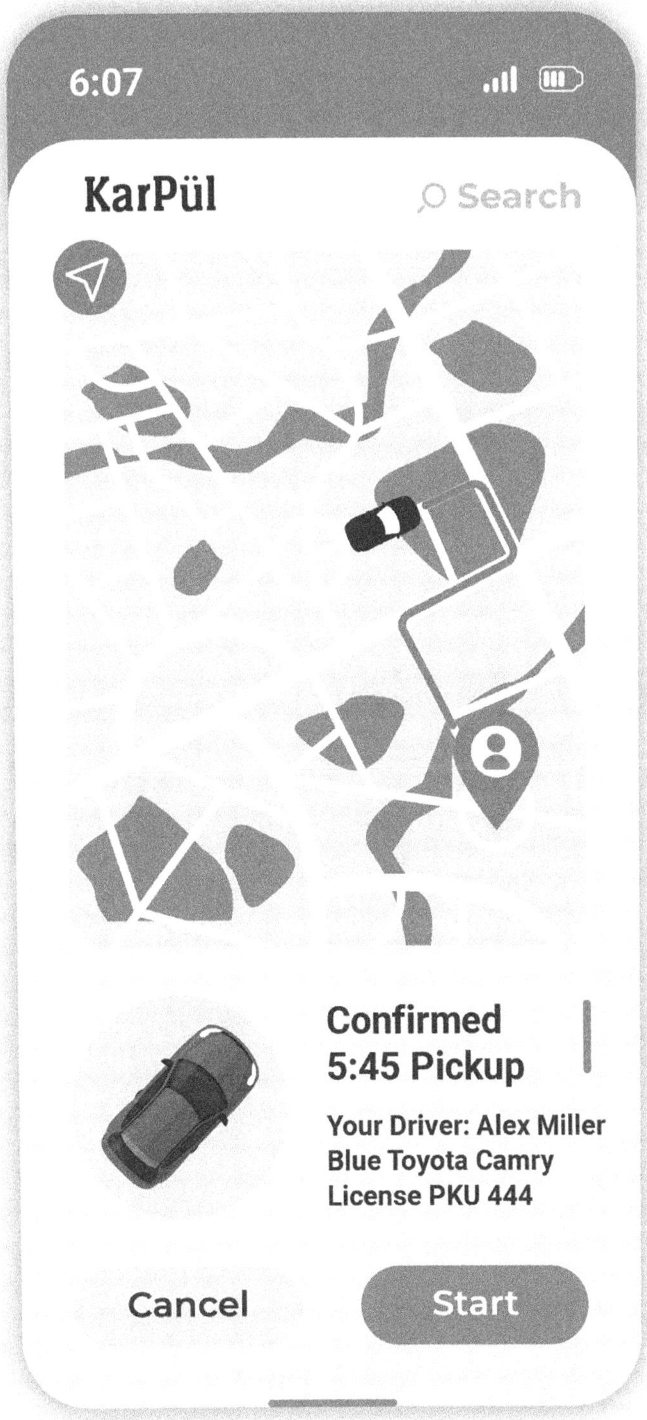

Exhibit 9

SUPPORTME SCREEN SHOT

SupportMe   Start a SupportMe   Share   About Us   DONATE

Miller Family Needs Your Help

$5,000 Goal

$3,541.00

DONATE NOW

	$50.00	**Lisa Stevens**
	$300.00	**Kyle Clarke**
	$100.00	**T. McGuiness**
	$100.00	**Jennifer Choi**

See All

Team fundraiser

Alex Miller, spouse, friend, child, former Army officer, needs our help. As many of you know, Alex's spouse Kai is undergoing treatment for aggressive thyroid cancer. Alex was working two jobs just to make ends meet and care for Kai. On September 4, Alex was working for KarPül and was involved in a car accident that was the direct fault of the other person involved in the accident. Alex was extremely shaken up by the event and has been unable to drive ever since. This leaves Alex with just one job and the Millers are going to be short in their rent payments. Please step up to help the Millers through this difficult time. I know that the Millers have been a support to each of you, now is our time to help them!

Exhibit 10

Resignation Email from Chen

From: Taylor Chen <t.chen@nunu.nita>
Sent: Feb 3, YR-1 11:33 AM
To: Max O'Brien <m.obrien@nunu.nita>
Subject: Resignation

Dear Max,

It is with deep regret that I have decided to resign from my position with NuNu Nectarine. As you know, I was involved in a car accident on September 4, YR-2. Since that time, I have been recovering from physical injuries and suffering from migraines related to those injuries. I was very hopeful to return to a full work schedule, but after trying to do so in November, I soon realized that the pace of the job was exacerbating my migraines. My doctor has advised that this may always be the case.

NuNu Nectarine has been my dream job. I feel that I have made a tremendous impact on its growth and success. I will miss being a part of the ride. However, I look forward to keeping in touch with all of you in the future.

Sincerely,

Taylor Chen

Exhibit 11

ALEX MILLER'S KARPÜL ACCIDENT REPORT

KarPül

Search

I was in an accident

At KarPül, we are committed to the safety of everyone using the KarPül platform – riders and drivers. If you were involved in an accident, please make sure that you and all parties are safe. Please notify the police and paramedics if necessary.

To help us understand what happened, please answer the following questions.

At the time of the accident:

Were you logged on to the KarPül app?

YES

Were you on your way to pick up a rider?

YES

Was a rider in your vehicle?

NO

Were any injuries reported? If so, describe.

YES, I hit a person that was walking in a crosswalk. I think the person had injuries to the head and to the leg. The person is in the hospital now. It seemed pretty bad.

Was your vehicle damaged? If so, describe.

NO

Today's Date: 9/5/YR-2

Date of Accident: 9/4/YR-2

Police Report:

Select file to upload

PDF

Anything else we should know about the accident:

There was a lot going on at the time of the accident. I was looking for my rider during rush hour traffic and I was running late for the pick up. I'm not sure whether or not the light was red in my direction. Since I was working at the time of the accident, I hope that KarPül can help me pay anything I might need to pay for hitting that pedestrian. I don't have the money.

Exhibit 12

Photographs of Miller's Car on September 5, YR-2

Exhibit 13

Street Photo

Exhibit 14

PHOTO OF BALLOONS

www.ingramcontent.com/pod-product-compliance
Lightning Source LLC
LaVergne TN
LVHW082352200926
848481LV00012B/3541
* 9 7 9 8 8 8 6 6 9 0 1 9 4 *